CHANGING CAREERS

AFTER THIRTY-FIVE

New Horizons
Through Professional
and Graduate Study

Changing Careers after Thirty-Five

New Horizons Through Professional and Graduate Study

DALE L. HIESTAND

Foreword by
ELI GINZBERG

1971

COLUMBIA UNIVERSITY PRESS
NEW YORK and LONDON

THIS REPORT was prepared for the Manpower Administration, U.S. Department of Labor, under research contract number 81-34-67-25 authorized by Title I of the Manpower Development and Training Act. Since contractors performing research under government sponsorship are encouraged to express their own judgment freely, the report does not necessarily represent the department's official opinion or policy. Moreover, the contractor is solely responsible for the factual accuracy of all material developed in the report.

Reproduction in whole or in part permitted for any purpose of the United States government.

To Wanda, My First Case

Foreword

PROFESSOR HIESTAND'S study of career changers—students over thirty-five in graduate or professional schools—opens up a new horizon in the studies of the Conservation of Human Resources Project at Columbia University of occupational choice and career development.

In its pioneering investigation of *Occupational Choice: An Approach to a General Theory* in 1951, the Conservation staff had assumed that the decision-making that people engage in with respect to their choice of a career extends through puberty and adolescence and continues even into young adulthood but that it is likely to result in the crystallization of a decision by the time they reach their early or their middle twenties. By that time their period of grace is at an end; they have completed an extended period of education and training preparatory to starting work or they have tried out certain jobs.

We had a few indications, however, that the process might not be so clean-cut. We recognized that occasionally a man who made an occupational decision and acted on it might find himself so dissatisfied after a few years at work that he would return to the university to continue his studies and prepare for an alternative career which he believed would more nearly fit his talents and values. We even designated his earlier decision as "pseudo-crystallization" because of its impermanence.

Our extended investigation into *The Ineffective Soldier: Lessons for Management and the Nation*, (3 vols.; 1959) led us to reconsider our earlier belief in the substantial irreversibility of the process of occupational choice. Many young men whose planning had been interrupted by the war and who were entitled to liberal GI benefits reopened the question of their occupational future when they were demobilized and set off on quite different directions.

Further confirmation that the process remains open much longer than we had originally estimated and was subject to redefinition and change during adulthood was provided by our study of *Talent and Performance* (1964), in which we traced fifteen to twenty years of work experience of a group of male fellowship winners. While the career pattern of most of this group was a more or less straightforward projection of their earlier choices and preparation, a considerable minority showed some degree of shift during their mature years.

Confirming and reinforcing this finding were the results that emerged from our study of the *Life Styles of Educated Women* (1966). This investigation revealed that a group of able women students whose careers we studied for one to two decades after their graduate studies contained many who shifted their fields of work, sometimes quite radically.

These several investigations had convinced us that, critical as are the years of adolescence and young adulthood for the formation and crystallization of an individual's occupational choice, it was essential to broaden the framework to make room for the changes that often take place in the mature years. And it is to this question particularly that Professor Hiestand's inquiry is directed.

Recognizing that individuals with considerable education and income are in a preferred position to consider a change in the nature of their careers in their mature years, Professor Hiestand selected for intensive study a group of persons already in or entering professional or managerial occupations. For the purposes of this analysis and for reasons that are outlined in chapter 1 he defined a career change as one that leads a person to return to graduate or professional school for at least one year of study after age thirty-five and after having been out of school long enough so that one could assume they were not still making their initial choice of a career field.

By virtue of his definition of a change in career and the selection of his group, Professor Hiestand was particularly concerned with higher education and its policies and practices with respect to older students. Many of his most pointed findings relate to these institutions' responses to the needs of the increasing number of older persons who seek admission or readmission.

In explaining the trend toward a higher proportion of older applicants seeking admission in connection with career changes, Professor Hiestand calls attention to such pervasive forces as the growth and transformation of professional work in the United States; the early completion of families; early retirement, optional and forced; the ability of many individuals to accumulate savings; the ability to work and study at the same time; and, perhaps most important, the desire of more and more men and women to lead more constructive and satisfying lives. While our forefathers had to devote most of their energies to making a place for themselves in the world of work and providing their children with a start in life, many in an affluent society can meet and surmount these basic challenges by the time they are in their forties. Hence they have the opportunity, if they so desire, to reshape and remold the second half of their working lives. For some, it is not a matter of choice or option but of necessity, since they find that they cannot continue in the same line of work. The lieutenant colonel who must retire from the Army after twenty years or the assistant vice-president whose firm has been merged and who finds himself without a job must make a job change and he may decide on a career change.

As is frequently the case with emergent problems, Professor Hiestand found that there is little information readily available about older graduate students, and less about those who return to school after they are thirty-five. Confronted with the absence of reliable facts and figures, Professor Hiestand decided to select a limited group for intensive study rather than to undertake a statistical inquiry. He selected a limited number of graduate institutions in the South, the Middle West, and the East, both governmental and private, and chose his sample from among their student bodies. He included both men and women and he did not limit the fields of study. His sample of seventy, with slightly more men than women, were distributed among sixteen disciplines or departments, from education which had the largest number (sixteen), to law and international studies which accounted for one apiece.

Professor Hiestand relied on three major bodies of materials which he assembled with the friendly cooperation of the university officials and the respondents. He collected data on applications, admissions, and attitudes of older students. Through interviews with academic and administrative officials he obtained a picture of the policies, practices, and experiences of the several institutions with older applicants and students. And, through an extended questionnaire, he elicited considerable information from his seventy respondents.

The rich information that Professor Hiestand collected and analyzed about the diverse reasons that people return to school preparatory to making a career change, the flexibility and suitability of admission and curriculum policies of the several institutions and departments in meeting the needs of older students, and the prospects of these older students of making a successful change upon completing their studies have justified his decision to use a case-study approach. Now that some of the critical issues in career changes in the middle years have been pursued and some of the major institutional potentialities and difficulties identified and evaluated, there is room for a comprehensive inquiry to determine the scale, scope, and significance of this increasingly important trend in manpower development and utilization in a technologically sophisticated and affluent economy.

In his final chapter, the author points up some of the major implications for manpower and educational policy from his exploratory study which warrant further research and evaluation. Among his important tentative conclusions are the following:

——Many educated men and women want to return to school and

in fact are returning to school as part of a process of changing their careers in the middle years. However, the size of this group, which is considerable and growing, should not be exaggerated.

——It is important from the viewpoint of guidance that many people who entertain the idea of returning to school or who in fact carry it through do so with relatively little prior planning or guidance.

——If more and more individuals in their middle years engage in career changes, including returning to school to effectuate them, it will become more important that young people in making their career plans recognize the need for a long-range strategy to provide for such an eventuality. This is particularly so for women who are likely to withdraw from the world of work for a considerable period of time while they devote themselves to raising their children.

——A dynamic economy creates manpower shortages. Too little attention has been paid to the possibility that older persons in the process of changing careers can meet these shortages. A beginning has been made to recruit some of them for high school and college teaching but the potentialities in the supply of older persons should be considered from a broader range.

——If more and more older persons return to school for advanced studies, added importance attaches to the quality of their basic education.

——The haphazard and prejudicial manner in which most institutions consider applications for admission from older students requires restudy and reform. A refusal to admit men and women older than a specified age to one or another type of program flatly denies their ability and the promise of later constructive performance both in school and in the world of work.

——Since education itself is a means of evaluating a person's motivation, capacity, and competence, the increasing demand of older persons for admission to institutions of higher learning points to the desirability of expanding educational facilities, particularly in urban communities and including opportunity for part-time study.

——The present formal requirements for entrance into higher education overwhelmingly based on a college degree warrant reappraisal in light of the emergence of junior and community colleges, special employer programs in-service and extra-mural, and the additional education that many adults obtain on their own. Graduate and professional schools should reappraise the additional education that many adults obtain.

——The return to school of many adults in the middle years is a dramatic manifestation of the changing structure and quality of these years. Middle age is no longer necessarily a period of hopes abandoned and of reconciliation prior to entering upon old age. It has become a period of new options that can provide an increasing number of men and women with new opportunities for developing new sources of satisfaction and meaning.

These are some of the more important lessons that Professor Hiestand has distilled from his exploratory study. The success of his effort is suggested by the rich agenda that he has developed for social scientists which should engage their attention and energies for a long time to come as they begin to direct themselves to probing more deeply into the long-neglected period of the middle years.

ELI GINZBERG, *Director*
Conservation of Human Resources Project
Columbia University

Acknowledgments

I WANT TO ACKNOWLEDGE the financial support of the Russell Sage Foundation and the United States Department of Labor for this project. I also want to thank Professor Eli Ginzberg for his advice and counsel on this study, as on so many other things. Professor Albert S. Thompson and Dr. Marcia Freedman were most helpful with comments on the entire manuscript, and it benefited greatly from the skilled editorial services of Ruth Szold Ginzberg. My able research assistants were Ruth Beinert and Paula Frank. Sylvia Leef and Mary Hagigeorgiou supervised the secretarial work.

I also must say a special word of thanks to the more than one hundred university and college presidents, vice-presidents, deans, directors, chairmen, professors, assistants, secretaries and employees who aided me at various stages in my interviews, case selection, and data collection. They will remain anonymous, but I learned from them at least as much about how institutions of higher education operate in general as I did about my specific topic. Special thanks for computer runs on their student records go to Mr. William Van Der Laan, Assistant Registrar of the University of Chicago, Professor Ralph B. Von Guerard, Registrar of New York University, and Mr. Charles B. Hurd, Registrar of Columbia University.

My deepest obligation is to those middle-aged students who responded to my case history questionnaire. My initial reservations about those who would abandon normal responsibilities for the never-never land of education and a new career in middle age were completely washed away by the enthusiasm, lively good sense, and optimism that the great majority of them evidenced. Characteristically, many of them thanked me for doing this study and thereby giving them voice.

DALE L. HIESTAND

Piermont, New York
October, 1970

Contents

CHANGING CAREERS
AFTER THIRTY-FIVE
New Horizons
Through Professional
and Graduate Study

1. Changing Careers and the Middle Years

BY POPULAR CONSENSUS, the middle years of life are expected to be a stable period of fulfillment. From an occupational vantage, we tend to view the middle years as a plateau, on the supposition that most people have attained their ambitions or have settled for less success than they had anticipated. The relatively small group of those who will continue to grow substantially in skill and responsibility after the age of forty have been fairly well identified, at least by their colleagues and superiors.

This assumption about stability is most commonly applied to those at the top of the social, educational, and occupational scale, namely those who have attended college and professional or graduate school and who are in professional or managerial occupations. Moreover, these occupations are generally considered closed to older persons who are lower on the scale on the premise that if educational or occupational opportunities are once missed, the exigencies of life make it impossible to recapture lost dreams or possibilities.

But we live in a dynamic and rapidly changing society and economy. Within a period as short as a decade, substantial changes occur in the attractiveness of particular fields of work, both to those already in them and to those who might enter them. Particular companies and public organizations wax and wane, and with them the attractiveness of particular jobs. Moreover, rapid changes take place in the content and working methods in the professions and management. This raises the specter of technological obsolescence, heretofore primarily a matter of concern to blue-collar workers. If we look more carefully, we see that many at the professional level are subject to more change than is commonly assumed. We soon see that significant numbers of persons are making substantial changes in the nature of their careers during middle age.

This study has been undertaken to explore the factors which encourage people to make or discourage them from making a significant change in the nature of their careers during middle age. We decided to gain some insight into this subject by studying those who seek to and do enter full-time or nearly full-time programs of professional or graduate study in middle age. Full-time study nearly always represents a significant break with one's past duties. It also presumably leads to the acquisition of major skills, permitting one or more of several different significant changes in the nature of one's career. First, education may enable one to enter a professional occupation for the first time. Second, full-time study may enable a person to make a substantial upward movement within a particular professional or career field. Third, full-time study may enable a person to enter a different, perhaps newly emerging, area of specialization within the general field in which he was previously engaged. Finally, full-time study at middle age may enable a person who is in one profession to enter a different profession. These four possibilities are four ways of changing the nature of one's career through education.

A substantial invasion of middle-aged students into professional and graduate schools for full-time study has occurred, apparently as the result of several ongoing fundamental changes in American society. First, the nature of professional and scientific occupations and of career patterns in these fields is changing. Second, fundamental changes seem to be under way in the character of middle age, particularly for persons with relatively high educational achievement, capabilities, and ambitions. These changes have been occurring for some time, and they now appear to be growing in importance. In the next several pages, we examine each of these developments more fully.

Changes in the nature of professional and scientific occupations and careers have occurred in a number of different ways. First, the rapid growth in the professional sector of the labor force has come about not so much through the growth of the more traditional professions, such as medicine, law, and the clergy, as through the emergence of new professions and fields. Increasingly, the professional occupations consist of a wide range of scientifically based occupations as well as of "helping" professions related to medical and social services and the like.

The second significant development in the professions has been the rapid rate of change in the content of particular fields. This in part reflects the increased extent to which the professions are based on research into the fundamental and applied sciences underlying fields and into the performance of particular professional functions, *per se*. Research thus produces new knowledge in particular fields and also changes the techniques and working methods in these fields. In addition, research often affects related professions as well as the fields in which it is being conducted. New knowledge and techniques in sociology, psychology, and economics are feeding into teaching, medical practice, social work, and management, while the findings of physics, chemistry, biology, and mathematics are absorbed into engineering, medical practice, and librarianship. The result has been not only to change the content of individual professions, but also to assist in the emergence of many new professions and specialties. Moreover, a considerable overlapping of the content of various professions has developed.

Third, along with these changes in structure and content, there have been changes in the nature of professional careers. Traditionally, a professional person worked alone and served nonprofessional clients, with loose relationships to his fellow professionals. Increasingly, however, engineers, scientists, and even lawyers function as parts of a larger group or enterprise, and increasing numbers are salaried employees. There has been a phenomenal rise in the number of professional people employed in profit-making organizations. There has been an even more phenomenal growth in the not-for-profit sector, which depends heavily on professional skills. With the notable exception of physicians, the careers of most professional personnel reflect geographical, vertical, and other kinds of mobility within their field. This has been encouraged by the growth of large aggregations of professional workers which in turn has encouraged the development of hierarchies, both for the performance of professional functions and for purposes of supervision.

Fourth, many professionals are now employed in other than the performance or administration of their profession's central function. Some are employed as educators in the profession, and there are many ancillary functions, such as the production of professional publications, work with professional associations, appraising grant applications, and representing the profession before other groups.

The growth and development of the professional sector, and especially the development of ranking systems and degrees of specialization, have opened up a wide range of hierarchical and promotional routes which help to structure professional careers. Thus, in the course of a career in a professional field, one often needs or acquires additional or different skills. These skills may be and often are acquired on the job or by independent study. However, in a modern society, they can often be acquired more efficiently in an educational institution. In addition, legal requirements and the tendency to place great faith in formal credentials often make it necessary or desirable for skills to be acquired in an educational institution rather than independently or on the job.

As the professional sector of the labor force has expanded, a steady transformation has occurred in the methods by which skills are acquired, both initially and in the course of a career. Of course, all professional skills were once acquired on the job in various forms of apprenticeship. Gradually, the acquisition of professional skills has moved out of the work place and into educational institutions. The result has been a rapid proliferation of professional and graduate programs for all sorts of specialties, including business administration, journalism, social psychology, operations research, etc. It is now conventional to define an occupation as a profession if most new entrants are required to have a college diploma in a particular curriculum. With few exceptions, post-baccalaureate study is now considered occupational in intent and therefore professional education by definition.

Formerly, once one had qualified for a profession, it was expected that he would be able to perform the functions of the profession for the remainder of his work life. If new skills were required, a professional person was able to acquire them by independent study or in the course of practice.

The assumption that initial professional education is adequate for a life time is increasingly in question. There has been a rapid growth in the demand for more formal means to acquire skills in middle age. There has been a veritable explosion of continuing education programs in the professions, with special institutes or programs ranging from an occasional hour to six months of full-time study. Post-doctoral or post-graduate education for professional persons is well established and rapidly growing. In this context, the possibility that full-time study for an extended period of time will be necessary or desirable for persons already in various professional fields is increasingly plausible.

These ongoing changes in the character of the professional occupations and in skill acquisition have been accompanied by important social changes affecting larger and larger numbers of people at middle age. Middle-aged people increasingly have options which were not formerly available to middle-aged people as a group, and not available to them as individuals when they were young. We will examine the factors tending to open up these options in turn.

For one thing, there seem to have been changes in the ages of adults at which important family events typically occur. Also, relationships within the family seem to be changing in character as does their timing. This is suggested by the phrase "early completion of families" but it is indeed, more complicated. Both women and men, particularly men, marry at an earlier age than formerly. The average age at marriage for young women is now twenty-one and for young men it is now twenty-two. It is no longer considered unusual for young students to marry while in college, and it is common for them to be married while in graduate or professional school. Those with professional ambitions may delay having children until they complete their education, but a great many do not. Moreover, the typical family contains no more than two or three children. It is commonplace that many housewives in their early thirties are free of the responsibility of child care during a substantial part of the day. As the years go by, they find themselves with more and more free time. Many women realize that they may well spend perhaps twenty to thirty years in paid employment after they reach thirty-five. In addition, the increasing importance of college and particularly graduate education means that the typical professional family is faced with financing the education of their children for a longer period of time. Given the greater income, freedom, and satisfaction in professional employment, there are increasing opportunities and incentives for women in their middle years to seek education that will enable them to enter or advance in those fields.

The early completion of families also has implications for men, the character of which is only beginning to emerge. For most professional men, a basic desire is to provide the style of life and the wherewithal to give their children an appropriate educational background. It is now possible for a successful man to provide for the college and postgraduate education of his children either out of current income or through savings at a fairly young age, say between forty and fifty. Having accomplished this, he may then consider seeking a new career, even in a field with lower pay scales.

Another factor increasing the options at middle age is that substantial numbers of people now have pension rights at a fairly young age. The most obvious example is the military, from which one can retire on a partial pension after twenty years of service or on full pension after thirty years of service. Thus, a military officer may retire with a substantial pension in his early forties. This principle applies to other occupations, notably those that are considered physically demanding. Moreover, reorganizations and mergers of industrial enterprises, which have been frequent in the past decade, are often followed by reductions in personnel, not only in the basic work force but also at the management and professional level. The release of personnel is sometimes made somewhat more graceful by altering the terms of pension plans so as to recompense employees for premature departure or to provide incentives for voluntary withdrawal. Pension payments may start much earlier than usual, either on a somewhat reduced basis, or at normal levels even without the full period of service. Such options create the possibility for many to retire from one employer and seek employment elsewhere, probably in another field, and thus to earn a second income and perhaps a second pension.

For a rather large proportion of people, middle age is marked by other events which may lead them, somewhat unexpectedly, to reconsider their employment and educational status in order to achieve a better, more satisfying life. In addition to those who are forced or induced to retire early, some find that their original career aspirations were not satisfied. If one's employer relocates his business, one must decide whether he wants to move with his employer to a new community or to stay in his present community and seek a new employer and career. The disruption of family life in connection with divorce, separation, or death of a spouse may lead people to return to school in the hope of establishing a more satisfactory life. It is commonplace that disruption of family life may make it necessary for a woman to return to work, possibly to school. Divorce or death of a spouse may mean a new type of life for men, too, leading them to reconsider their career and educational choices even in the absence of economic need.

Again, one who never marries may only slowly begin to take that fact into account. A man or a woman entering middle age may well have accumulated substantial savings if he or she has had a reasonably satisfactory career. In the gradual reappraisal of his life, a single middle-aged person may decide in favor of a new career which requires professional training.

Another significant factor in reopening fundamental career choices is the high level of political instability in many parts of the world. The United States has received and continues to receive a succession of refugee groups from Eastern Europe, Latin America, the Near East, and Asia. Frequently, the structure, content, and educational requirements of an occupation in a refugee's former country is different from that in the United States, and his skills are not appropriate or his credentials are not accepted here. For a refugee, a period in school may be necessary or attractive, as a means either to be certified in his profession or to train for a new one.

For significant numbers of Americans, the middle years are a period during which skills, interests, and options continue to develop. We have noted that this may result from a desire to maintain or improve oneself in a professional field which is growing and changing. When they were young, many were not aware of their potential or of the opportunities which would develop for them. As a result of continued development and exposure to an ever-widening and ever more interesting world, an evolution and crystallization of new ambitions occurs for some. Those who were earlier satisfied with being journeyman professionals may develop higher aspirations. Those who were satisfied to enter a profession as general practitioners may gradually become interested in becoming specialists. Those who sought to satisfy their psychological and social needs in one way may gradually become aware of better and more gratifying ways to satisfy those needs. Those who worked in a field primarily for income while they satisfied their deeper interests in an avocation may gradually discover that, as a practical matter, these interests can be satisfied in a paying occupation.

One common assumption is that the person who returns to school is attempting to realize frustrated ambitions. This is indeed a possibility, and many do satisfy their youthful ambitions after entering middle age. It is also possible that success in one's early ambitions can lead to a search for new fields to conquer. Returning to school in order to go more deeply into a field or to enter a new field may well provide the best way to maintain a high level of satisfaction in one's life.

The drive for new skills at middle age may also reflect fundamental changes in general attitudes among Americans. Many have commented on the disillusionment among young people with the business and commercial world. Widely shared attitudes of the young often have their precursor in the ill-formed attitudes of their parents.

Finally, there seems to be a new attitude on the part of society in general toward those in middle age, and middle-aged persons particularly seem to be developing new attitudes toward themselves. These attitudes favor a far greater degree of freedom for the middle-aged. Once it would have been considered unusual, indeed odd, to encounter a middle-aged person as a student in a college or university. Increasingly, however, we find middle-aged students in a variety of part-time and full-time programs of general education, remedial education, and advanced professional training. The right of middle-aged men and women to change their minds about what they want out of life may well be emerging. In short, the right of these persons to find satisfaction in their work and in their lives is increasingly recognized. These increased rights are both the cause and the result of the increased need for and the financial capacity to seek added skills, but they also mean that middle-aged persons find increasing support for their efforts to overstep former boundaries in the search for personal satisfaction.

The result of these fundamental changes in the professional and scientific occupations and in the character of middle age is that substantial numbers of persons are now making significant changes in the nature of their careers and occupations. This study was undertaken to explore some of the factors involved when the individuals do in fact decide to enter a new career field or to make a substantial change in the nature of their careers if they stay in the same field.

For the purposes of this study, we decided to equate entry into a new career or a substantial change in the nature of one's career with enrolling in professional or graduate school after age of thirty-five for full-time study for at least one year or for a part-time schedule which would permit the equivalent of a year of full-time study to be accomplished in no more than two years. To count as a change in career, we required that this study period be preceded by significant work experience, or, for women, by time out of school. We did not include those whose study was continuous, as with medical specialists or those who have continually moved from school to school. For either, continued attendance at school might more properly be considered a part of their first choice of career fields.

The choice of full- or nearly full-time study as a criterion of shift in occupational field or in the nature of one's career was based on the presumption that a year or more of full-time professional study produces a substantial change in the nature and level of one's skills. When one enters study on a full-time basis well past the conventional age for going to professional or graduate school, it surely represents a major decision about the nature of one's future employment. In light of the lack of or reduction in employment and income, the redirection of interest, and the fundamentally different requirements that a student must meet, we can assume that attending school for a year or more means that major additions to skills will be made.

While not all who make a significant change in the nature of their careers return to school on a full-time or nearly full-time basis, careful research about a group of middle-aged students should provide some understanding of what is involved when persons do make substantial shifts in the nature of their employment without reentering school. It is true, of course, that returning to school for a year or more may in fact produce no change in the nature of a person's career. This is possible, but it does not seem likely. Even if one returns to precisely the same job, his added skills almost surely will lead to a change in the nature of his performance.

One may ask why the age of thirty-five is used as the criterion for "middle age." For most purposes, an individual who is thirty-five years old is not quite middle-aged. Most people, however, have completed their education and have established their careers or positions in work, their homes, and their families by age thirty-five. To be sure, establishment in a career or job does not always follow immediately upon completing college or graduate school. Each year, a certain number of graduates reenter school after a year or more of employment because they have decided that the field they originally selected will not provide a satisfactory career for them. Others shift their fields without having made what appears to be a firm choice of occupation by age thirty-five. There is no doubt in the minds of most college or university students that a student aged thirty-five is "older." Since the occupational lives of some professionals last from, say, twenty-five to sixty-five, occupational old age must start at about fifty or fifty-five. Indeed, by some definitions, anyone over forty-five is an "older" worker. In this light, thirty-five years of age seems to be a reasonable dividing line, not young with regard to a future career and relatively old for admission as a student.

This discussion of changes in careers and occupations in middle age will benefit from reference to some of the findings which emerged during the course of our study. It is conceivable, and occasionally it happens, that a person moves from one field to another, fundamentally different, field. Our investigations, however, indicate that this is quite unusual. Most persons who move from one field to another have a certain set of skills, experiences, attitudes, and approaches which substantially aid them in their new occupations. Our research suggests that it is highly unusual for a person to abandon totally a decade or more of experience in one field to strike out in a completely new direction.

A common pattern is that one upgrades his skills substantially, making it possible to move from one level of performance to a distinctly new level of performance in the same field. An example is an engineer with a master's degree who returns to school to study for a Ph.D. in order to engage in fundamental research. Another is the nurse who returns for an advanced degree in order to undertake administrative functions.

Another pattern could be called "the 45° turn." Often a professional person acquires new skills which enable him to move into a new, related field or a highly specialized part of his present field which can be defined as a distinctly new profession. An example is a public health nurse who decides to become a social worker. Another is a social worker who returns to school for the training necessary to become a psychiatric social worker. Or, an economist who reenters graduate school to become a mathematical economist, and later returns to become a mathematician. In some cases a new career field is an outgrowth of a long-run avocational interest which is gradually converted into a career field.

Another significant pattern of career changing is when a man keeps working in his first field while he slowly builds a position in a second. The risk of changing career fields is so great that some continue working at their first profession while studying and even working part time in a new profession. One example is a naval officer approaching retirement who asked for shore duty and then deliberately sought out teaching assignments in order to test his interest and ability to become a professor of business subjects. When he retired from the Navy, he became a full-time teacher and a part-time student. Finally, he returned to school full time. Similarly, a housewife might take a part-time job in a particular field to test her interest in it preparatory to returning to school. At first, she might study as a part-time and later as a full-time student. The end result may well be a full-time commitment to work in this field.

We should note that there has been developed in this country a vast system of part-time or continuing education. The number of people who go to college and university on a part-time or inter-mittent basis, including teachers, physicians, engineers, and others, is substantial and constantly increasing. Great numbers are signifi-cantly enhancing their skills and therefore are significantly chang-ing the level of their performance within a career field. Indeed, some are slowly transforming their career interests from one field to another. Because this kind of education leads only to slow and evolutionary changes in careers—and because many who par-ticipate do not make significant changes—those who change by this slow process have not been included for study here.

The following chapters are organized around three different kinds of information which we obtained during this study. First, an attempt was made to collect data on applications, admissions, and attendance at professional and graduate schools by men and women aged thirty-five or over with particular attention to varia-tions among different professions and disciplines. The results of that investigation are presented in chapter 2.

Second, a questionnaire was sent to a number of persons who had entered or reentered professional or graduate school after age thirty-five. Their reasons for returning to school are explored in chapter 3.

Third, information on policies, practices, and experiences of professional and graduate schools with respect to older applicants and students was obtained from interviews with various school and university officers. The interviews covered admissions, finan-cial aid, academic performance, and other aspects of attendance of older students. The results of that investigation appear in chapter 4.

In chapter 5, we return to information gained from the question-naire and discuss the process of entering, attending, and leaving school from the older individual's point of view, including how these persons reached their decisions, the preparations they made, their educational and other experiences in school, the impact of study on family life, and their subsequent return to work.

Chapter 6 presents a series of case histories to illustrate the complexity of the individual decisions and of the action patterns in returning to school. Chapter 7 discusses the implications of the present study for manpower and educational policy.

2. Fields of Study

IN THIS CHAPTER, we will consider the relative importance of middle-aged persons among professional and graduate students in total and in various fields of study. We had hoped to obtain data on applications by and admissions of middle-aged students, in addition to actual attendance at professional and graduate schools. Unfortunately, few schools or departments in universities have information on applications and admissions by age, except on the individual student records.

The best we could obtain were the ages of students currently enrolled; therefore our data include those who reached age thirty-five while they were in school as well as those who entered or reentered after that age. The inclusion of persons who entered prior to age thirty-five is probably relatively more frequent in the data on Ph.D. students than it is in the case of students in master's programs and professional schools. In the latter nearly all students progress directly through course work and finish in a limited period of time. In Ph.D. programs, oral examinations and dissertations often elongate the period of study. In recent years, however, the increases in financial support available to students and the increased pressures from faculties may be tending to shorten the period of Ph.D. study. Of course, depending upon school policies, many Ph.D. candidates not in residence are not included in enrollment statistics.

Our sources of information about the ages of enrolled professional and graduate students include a few national samples of graduate students collected in other studies plus data we collected in 1967 from a limited number of universities. We found only three universities with computerized records in sufficient detail for our purposes. These three were the University of Chicago, New York University, and Columbia University. Unfortunately, the Chicago data do not distinguish between full-time and part-time students. The New York University data do not distinguish among the various departments within the Graduate School of Arts and Sciences. Only Columbia was able to provide data according to all the classifications that seemed useful to us: year of birth, sex, department and school, and enrollment as a full- or part-time student. Even Columbia had only fragmentary data on Teachers College, which functions as the university's graduate school of education, but with a separate charter. Universities were just beginning to put data on students and admissions into the computer at the time we were gathering data, and much more and better data will surely be available in the future.

The proportion of graduate and professional students who are thirty-five years old or older varies from one study to another, largely because each study includes a somewhat different mixture of graduate and professional students. In his national sample of graduate students in 1958-59, James Davis found that 9.5 percent were over thirty-five.[1] In his sample, which included both full- and part-time students, older students were found less frequently among full-time students. Warkov, Frisbie, and Berger found that 15 percent of the graduate students in their 1963 survey were thirty-five or older.[2] Their data also included both full-time and part-time students, but they did not include those in programs in elementary and secondary education. We found no earlier com-

[1] James Davis, *Stipends and Spouses* (Chicago, University of Chicago Press, 1962), p. 170.

[2] Seymour Warkov, Bruce Frisbie, and Alan S. Berger, *Graduate Student Finances, 1963*, NORC Report No. 103 (Chicago, 1965). See Appendix Table 1.

prehensive data on the ages of graduate and professional students.[3]

We found that in 1966 older students comprised 16.5 percent of all professional and graduate students in New York University, 20.4 percent in Columbia University including Teachers College, 10.3 percent at Columbia University proper, and 8.7 percent at the University of Chicago. Of the full-time professional and graduate students alone, those aged thirty-five or older represented 3.7 percent at N.Y.U. and 5.4 percent at Columbia proper. These figures are not completely comparable, but they indicate the relative proportions. If we also take account of the fact that some of the part-time students, probably a minority, are taking a relatively heavy schedule, it appears that at least 7 percent of the professional and graduate students attending these universities on a full-time or nearly full-time basis were thirty-five or over. Since these and similar institutions dominate professional and graduate education, other than for teachers, and since teacher-education tends to attract relatively large numbers of middle-aged students, we would expect the proportion of all full-time or nearly full-time professional and graduate students in the country who are thirty-five and over to be at least 6 percent, and perhaps as high as 7 percent.

The proportions differ greatly among departments and between men and women. Appendix Tables 1 to 7 present detailed tables based on the 1963 survey of graduate students by Warkov, Frisbie, and Berger for the National Opinion Research Center and the data we obtained from the three universities. The remainder of this chapter generalizes from these tables and from the subjective and fragmented reports received in our interviews with university and school officials.

Obviously, a great range of factors affect the proportions who are middle-aged among the students in various departments and

[3] Nor did Pins, who wrote his study of social work students prior to the publication of Davis' study. See Arnulf M. Pins, *Who Chooses Social Work, When and Why?* (New York, Council on Social Work Education, 1963), p. 60.

schools of universities. On the one hand, the proportions depend on the decisions made by those who are potential students, and the objective and subjective factors which influence older and younger persons in making these decisions may differ among fields. On the other hand, the proportions of middle-aged students in the various fields reflect in part the policies and practices of educational institutions and officials. These two subjects will be considered more fully in chapters 3 and 4. Here, we can introduce comments suggesting cause and effect relationships in only a tentative way.

In general, the proportion of all female professional and graduate students who are thirty-five or older is about twice the proportion among male students. Thus, among male full-time graduate and professional students, 2.5 percent at N.Y.U. and 4.1 percent at Columbia proper were thirty-five or over, while the percentages were 6.4 and 9.1, respectively, for full-time women students. However, women account for 30 to 40 percent of all students past thirty-five in the professional and graduate programs of these universities, and for about half of the older full-time students.

We obtained fragmentary evidence which suggests that men who return to graduate or professional school on a full-time basis tend to do so somewhat earlier than do women. In the data for some schools, we found a relatively higher number of men between the ages of thirty-five and thirty-nine, a somewhat smaller number between the ages of forty and forty-five, and relatively few men older than forty-five. For women, however, the number is likely to be higher between the ages of forty and forty-five than between thirty-five and thirty-nine. Significant numbers of women return to full-time graduate study in their late forties or in their fifties, and a few in their sixties.

There are important differences among fields in the proportion of older students. While significant numbers of older *part-time* students are found in engineering, very few older *full-time* students are found in engineering, mathematics, or the natural sciences. Within the natural sciences, practically no older students are found in the physical sciences, such as chemistry and physics, but modest proportions are found among the students in the geological and biological sciences.

The relatively few older full-time students in the physical sciences, mathematics, and engineering is consistent with the fact that these fields, particularly engineering, lose rather than gain students as an age group passes through college and later work careers. Other divisions of a university typically receive transfers from the engineering and physical science divisions each year. Moreover, those who are trained and employed as engineers and scientists soon begin to disperse themselves throughout the organizations which they enter. Although there is some inward flow from other fields, it is relatively limited.

Most educators are aware of the phenomenon of the relatively few middle-aged full-time students in the physical sciences and engineering. In these fields, technology and content change rapidly, and concern about technological obsolescence is prevalent. In these fields, therefore, a great deal of continuing and on-the-job education is directed at overcoming this threat of obsolescence. In these fields, moreover, high performance seems to come more often from the young. One might speculate that these are highly theoretical fields where the content is highly integrated in a developmental sense, and where materials and concepts have to be learned in a more or less rigid sequence. If one were to enter an engineering or mathematics program at middle age, he would have to retake some subjects that are normally covered at adolescence or during the early years of college. This may so stretch out the process of reentering that it is not feasible.

There tend to be relatively few older full-time students in the traditional professions of medicine, law, dentistry, and nursing. The Association of American Medical Colleges reports that those past thirty-five account for less than 2 percent of their students. There tend to be many older part-time law students, but not many are full time. A few older nurses are found entering specialties such as nursing education, public health, and the like. Among medical specialties, psychoanalysis and public health represent an exception, and they have been considered traditional "second career" fields for some physicians.

The largest proportions of older students tend to be found in service professions, including social work, library service, secondary and elementary education, and various kinds of psychological and mental health services. In these fields, training programs are relatively short. The skills and concepts are drawn from psychology, sociology, information science, and other less rigidly structured disciplines. It may be that an older person can move into these fields somewhat more easily because his experience, maturity, reading, and general professional preparation are relevant, and professional education can be a matter of filling in for his weaknesses. Even here, we have discovered that there are some problems of technological obsolescence. For instance, social work students are expected to have a background of sociology. A middle-aged returnee quite often finds that the content of sociology has changed while he was out of school.

Finally, we have discovered a significant proportion of middle-aged students in Ph.D. programs leading to college teaching in the social sciences and humanities. The subject matter of these fields, of course, is popular and read avocationally by many people. Many governmental and business officials read widely in those social sciences relevant to their work. College teaching seems attractive to many of these avocational and general readers. Admissions officers spend a great deal of time trying to make clear the difference between avocational or general interests in these subjects and their pursuit as an academic discipline. Undoubtedly the point is often well made and many would-be applicants are discouraged. On the other hand, the openness of these fields plus the high degree of interest that they hold for a great many persons may be why they tend to have relatively large numbers of middle-aged students.

There seem to be significant numbers of older students in foreign languages and studies. Many of these are refugees who want to capitalize on their experiences and backgrounds and become teachers in a university, college, junior college, or high school in this country.

In general, the data suggest that in the natural sciences, mathematics, engineering, and the like, the proportion of older full-time students tends to be less than 5 percent and indeed often is less than 1 percent. On the other hand, in leading graduate humanities and social sciences programs, the proportion of older students tends to fall within the range of 5 to 10 percent, but it is sometimes higher, especially in the languages. In such professional programs as education, library service, social work, religion, and the like, 10 percent would be a small proportion, and proportions of 20 percent or greater are not uncommon. In his national study of full-time first year students in schools of social work, Pins found that 12 percent of the men and 21 percent of the women, or 18 percent of all students, were thirty-five or older.[4] The highest ratios we found in sizable professional schools were at Columbia's Schools of Library Service and Public Health, where a third of the full-time students were thirty-five or older.

The service professions thus tend to account for the greater number of older students. At N.Y.U., 65 percent of the full-time older professional and graduate students were in education and social work. At Columbia proper, 25 percent were in social work and library service.

It is evident that the proportions of older students, both male and female, tend to be higher in fields associated with women rather than in those associated with men. It may be that men and women who seek education at middle age are simply more oriented to traditionally "female" professions. However, it may be due to more fundamental factors. The fact that "female" fields tend to have relatively short training periods may be a significant factor in the recruitment of middle-aged men as well as women. Moreover, the

[4]Pins, p. 31.

fields which are associated with women tend to be those with relatively severe manpower shortages. Educators may be more willing to accept middle-aged applicants in that case. These fields also tend to offer relatively generous stipends or fellowships which are attractive to middle-aged persons with responsibilities. Finally, the leaders in many fields associated with women are trying to recruit larger numbers of men. As a result, middle-aged men who apply for admission to graduate programs in these fields may be more readily accepted.

Our interviews in each metropolitan area gave us the strong impression that there is a tendency for higher proportions of older full-time students to be found in the nationally famous universities, rather than in those identified with the local areas. This contrasts with the report by Davis that "older [graduate] students are more common in lower-stratum schools."[5] However, his definition of older students were those aged twenty-seven or older, and the large majority in his sample were part-time students, presumably including a large proportion of teachers going to local institutions to build up credits in order to get into a higher salary grade. It may be that most older potential full-time students want only the best and are not willing to take the risk and sacrifice of quitting work to go to school full time at a lesser-ranked school. By and large, moreover, we found little evidence of full-time middle-aged students in suburban universities. While there were a significant number of middle-aged students at some Catholic universities, others had very few. The older students at Catholic universities included a relatively high proportion of priests and nuns.

We found little evidence that many Negroes are involved in the return to full-time education after age thirty-five. This is particularly true at those institutions which tend to have relatively high proportions of Negro students, such as the Negro universities in the South and the urban public universities in the North. On the other hand, Edwards reports that Negroes who become profes-

[5] James Davis, p. 30.

sionals enter and complete professional training "somewhat later than is the case for white professionals."[6] In his study of Negro professionals employed in Washington, D.C., in the 1950s, he found that 16 percent had received their degrees at age thirty-five or older, and 2 percent at age forty or older. The proportion receiving their degree at age forty or older came to 12 percent among teachers with the Ph.D.; 2 percent for lawyers, dentists, and teachers with an M.A.; and only 1 percent for physicians. However, these figures do not appear to be out of line with those for all students presented earlier. It may be that, with relatively smaller proportions of the Negro population entering professional and graduate education, those who are thirty-five or older can hardly fail to be a relatively small number. It may also be that, among middle-aged persons from backgrounds in which college education alone represents a major achievement, few will be so adventurous or dissatisfied that they will set out on a new course of study at middle age.

In summary, older full-time students are equally divided between the sexes, they are more likely to be at the leading universities, and they tend to be in the helping professions, social sciences, or humanities. Their numbers are too few to transform the university student body. However, they are a significant proportion of all professional and graduate students, large enough to give a different flavor to a significant number of departments and schools in universities. Why they have returned to school and the nature of their reception and experience in school are the subjects of the next chapters. This will cast additional light on the phenomenon of changing careers in the middle years.

[6] G. Franklin Edwards, *The Negro Professional Class* (Glencoe, Free Press, 1959), p. 158.

3. Why Return to School?

THIS CHAPTER will explore the reasons which impel a person aged thirty-five or older to return to professional or graduate school on a full-time or nearly full-time basis. It is based on a group of case histories obtained from present and former students in a variety of institutions of higher education in four metropolitan areas—New York, Chicago, St. Louis, and Nashville. These cities were arbitrarily selected, but they include the two largest urban educational complexes as well as middle-size Midwestern and Southern cities. Approximately one-fourth of all professional and graduate students in the United States are in these four metropolitan areas.

In the course of our visits to schools and universities to discuss their older applicants and students, we asked educational administrators to provide the names of a number of students who had entered or reentered after age thirty-five. We had little control over the selection of the individuals in more than half the institutions, schools, and departments, although we were sometimes able to exercise some control over the distribution among departments and schools in a university. In other institutions, schools, and departments, we had access to files containing students' names and birth dates. and we could select our own cases. Wherever we had information about the department or school, sex, and other characteristics of older students, we sought a sample which was roughly representative. It was easy to find older students in education and social work and consequently we made greater efforts to find students from other fields. We also selected proportionately more from the smaller cities.

The possibility of other biases in the selection process exists.

Departmental chairmen, deans, or their secretaries may have tended to select outstanding or unusual older students. About half of those to whom we sent our questionnaire responded. Nearly two hours were required to fill out the questionnaire and many were too busy with school or work to do so.

In the end, we worked with a group of seventy respondents. Thirty-nine had gone to institutions and around New York City, eighteen in the Chicago area, nine in the St. Louis area, and four in the Nashville area. However, since each of these educational centers draws from a wide region, even from the entire nation, the group has a broader geographical base than at first appears.

In our group, as Table 3.1 indicates, there were forty men and

TABLE 3.1. *Sex and Marital Status of Respondents*

	Male	*Female*	*Total*
Single	7	7	14
Married	31	18	49
Remarried	2	1	3
Divorced	0	4	4
Total	40	30	70

thirty women. One-fifth had never married, which is a higher proportion than obtains in the total population. Four of the women were divorced, and two men and one woman had remarried after widowhood or divorce.

When these students returned to school, the students ranged in age from thirty-five to fifty-eight (Table 3.2). The men tended to be somewhat younger than the women: median ages were forty-one and forty-five, respectively. Only three men and seven women were fifty years of age or over.

The men differed significantly from the women in both the degrees they held and the degrees they were seeking. Only two of the men, but eight of the women, had no degree (Table 3.3). Four of the men already held doctorates, but none of the women did.

TABLE 3.2.   *Age of Older Students on Entering or Reentering Professional or Graduate School, by Sex*

Age	Males	Females
35 to 39	16	8
40 to 44	12	6
45 to 49	9	9
50 to 54	2	4
55 to 59	1	3
Total	40	30

TABLE 3.3.   *Highest Degree Held on Reentering School and Degree Program Entered, by Sex*

	Highest Degree Held Prior to Return		Degree Program Entered	
Degree	Men	Women	Men	Women
None	2	8	1	1
Bachelor's or first professional	20	13	2	8
Master's	14	9	17	16
Doctorate	4	—	20	5
Total	40	30	40	30

Fully half of the men entered doctoral programs, while more than half of the women entered master's programs. Even if we eliminate the women who had no college degrees, less than one-fourth entered doctoral programs. In middle age, as in youth, the goals of women seem markedly lower than those of men.

More than one-fifth of the respondents were entering programs in education (Table 3.4). The next largest group were those in graduate business programs, all of whom were men. Social work, library service, and health service accounted for nearly one-fifth of the respondents, and most of these were women. Languages, literature, and linguistics accounted for another significant group, again largely women. On the other hand, the diverse social sciences

TABLE 3.4. *Field of Study Undertaken on Entering or Reentering Professional or Graduate School, by Sex*

Field	Men	Women	Total
Education	7	9	16
Business	7	—	7
Social work	1	5	6
Library service	2	3	5
Health service	1	1	2
Religion	2	—	2
Law	1	—	1
English language and English–American literature	—	5	5
Other languages and literature	3	1	4
Anthropology	2	1	3
Psychology	2	3	5
History	2	2	4
Political science	3	—	3
International studies	1	—	1
Mathematics	3	—	3
Engineering and physical sciences	3	—	3
Total	40	30	70

and history provided a group as large as those entering education, and most of these were men. An unusually high number of the respondents were undertaking advanced study in mathematics, engineering, or the physical sciences.

The remainder of this chapter is devoted to the question of *why* these persons in or approaching middle age decided to enter or reenter professional or graduate school for full-time or nearly full-time study. Determining why people do what they do is always difficult, of course. For any person, there are always many kinds of explanations. One can explain the actions of an individual in terms of a social force, practical reasons, or even the deepest psychological factors. Even within these general categories of explanations, there is nearly always a variety of intersecting influences attracting, persuading, propelling, or forcing a person to make a particular decision. At the same time, there are always other, weaker factors which might have forestalled this particular step or led to some other step.

We rely upon the reasons offered by the respondents in answer to the following question:

A man or woman may enter or reenter professional or graduate training in the middle years for a variety of reasons: his interests and ambitions may change or develop; he may want to improve himself; he may have been more or less forced into it; or new opportunities may have opened up due to changes in the funds available, family or work responsibilities, and the like.

Please discuss your own reasons in some detail, indicating (in more specific terms than those used above) the factors which led you to enter or reenter graduate or professional training at a much later age than usual. Also indicate any negative factors which you had to weigh in reaching your decision to return to school.

This question was followed by two pages of lined spaces, an open invitation for an extended essay. Most of the respondents fully used these pages.

The reasons for returning to school suggested above provide one basis for tabulating the responses. These reasons are not all at the same level of generality; some represent positive forces, others negative forces, and still others facilitating factors. However, the responses to an open-ended enquiry typically differ in these ways. As Table 3.5 indicates, the seventy respondents provided a total of 194 separate reasons, or nearly three reasons per person.

The preponderance of the responses offered could be classified as developmental. Over half of the respondents made some statement which indicated that their return was due at least in part to the development of their interests. Over a third indicated that the continued development of their ambitions played a role. Nearly a third indicated a desire to improve themselves intrinsically, as distinct from matters of ambition.

TABLE 3.5. *Reasons for Returning to School*

Reason	Number of respondents
A change in interests	13
A change in ambitions	17
Development of interests	38
Development of ambitions	27
Successful in former activities	9
To improve self intrinsically	21
Forced into it	8
Funds available from others	14
Personally financially able	12
Reduced family responsibilities	10
Other	25
Total responses	194

Nearly half indicated that their return to school was due to significant changes in their ambitions or interests. However, very few suggested that their return was in any way forced. The availability of funds from others or from their own savings or current income was cited by over a third. Only a third of the women stated that their return was due essentially to a reduction in family responsibilities.

This tabulation was based on the list of possible reasons suggested to the students. Examination of the written responses themselves suggested a different list of reasons. In developing this list, we concentrated on what appeared to be the primary factor which led each individual to reenter school. In an open-ended discursive response, of course, it is often difficult to identify the primary reason. Sometimes, it seemed to us that a factor which was not even mentioned directly by the respondent was primary. However, we relied heavily upon the actual words and emphases of each respondent to reach a conclusion as to the primary reason. In many cases, the primary reason was quite clear because of the respondent's emphasis or his explicit ranking of several reasons.

Those who had been housewives presented us with an interesting problem. It is now common for housewives to turn to other types of activities some time after age thirty-five. We did not think a desire to turn to nonhomemaking functions an adequate reason for entering a program of higher education. In a great many cases, the decision to seek activity outside the home is essentially separate from the decision to enter an institution of higher education, for nearly every housewife has other options. Of course, motivation and impelling factors are always intertwined and difficult to separate. However, we tried to distinguish those reasons which led a woman to seek activity outside the home from those which led her to an institution of higher education. In a few cases, this did not suffice, as will become evident below.

The respondents tended to answer from a personal or individualistic point of view and rarely made reference to sociological factors. Most respondents avoided psychological reasons or rationales for their behavior. Even the psychologists tended to avoid psychological responses, either because they believed that we did not want such a response or because they preferred to provide more conventional responses. For instance, one psychologist, after discussing objective events which led to his entering a quite new career field and indicating how and why various aspects of the work were meaningful to him, remarked, "There is much more that I could say in connection with the above motivation to work with children, schools, and parents. If you care for more of the same, please let me know."

By a loose grouping of the primary reasons offered by the respondents, we can indicate the relative importance of various factors in leading these middle-aged persons to enter or reenter graduate or professional school. As Table 3.6 indicates, the largest group placed primary emphasis on their intrinsic interest in the subject matter, field of study, or field of work. For instance, a former assistant vice-president of a bank reported that he found himself increasingly involved in educational activities and began

TABLE 3.6. *Primary Reasons for Entering or Reentering Professional or Graduate School, by Sex*

	Total	Male	Female
Intrinsic interest in subject or field	16	7	9
To acquire new or increasingly important skills in present field	6	5	1
To realize an earlier ambition	2	1	1
To improve financial status	2	1	1
To acquire necessary credentials or skills	9	6	3
Available support, funds, fellowship, etc.	11	7	4
Affluence or financial capacity	5	4	1
Change desirable or necessary	14	6	8
Other	5	3	2
Total	70	40	30

to reflect upon his own "enthusiasm and sense of accomplishment" as a part-time teacher, part-time student, and member of a board of education. "It became increasingly evident that my contacts with the educational field were in many ways more rewarding (nonpecuniary) than my professional career." With a bachelor's degree in mathematics and an M.B.A. obtained through part-time study over eleven years, he entered a Ph.D. program in finance and accounting.

A college dropout who became business manager of an auto dealership reported, "I became aware of my own scholastic short-coming [when I] attempted to help my son in his high-school work." He reentered college as a part-time student at age forty-five to complete a bachelor's program in business administration. He then "became interested in the educational process itself." His grades were excellent, he received considerable encouragement from an economics instructor, and he enrolled in a Ph.D. program in economics when he received his bachelor's degree.

Another case was a young woman who reentered college at age thirty-one to get a bachelor's degree in education and who slowly began to realize the nature of her capacities and opportunities. As a result, she continued for a master's degree in English at age thirty-four, and later, after obtaining a divorce, entered a Ph.D. program in English. Similarly, a 50-year-old elementary school teacher with only a normal school certificate "decided to take a 'course.' Something clicked and I made up two years in one and taught at the same time. I had a 4.8 out of 5 average, which made me happy. I love everything about the university—the people, the learning, etc." She next completed a master's degree in nine months while teaching full time. At last word she plans to enter a doctoral program, hoping and expecting to finish in two years. A similar case is an electrical engineer who, after being assigned to buying electrical equipment, decided to take a few law courses because he needed the background. After one semester of part-time study, he reported, "I was hooked and wished that I could have done it twenty years sooner." He completed the equivalent of a regular three-year program in six years part time and was later promoted to senior buyer in his department.

In other cases, scholarly interests were triggered by part-time study. A housewife, a foreign national resident in the United States because of her husband's work, had earlier studied law, theology, and social work in Europe. After some time in the United States she determined to get a "good" degree in liberal arts as a part-time student. "Just before that first semester began I went to [the] library and sat down there with the book I had picked out. (It was Kant.) Then I knew I never would leave it anymore. . . . A whole new world, which I had not even realized existed, slowly opened. . . . Halfway up the mountain . . . I began to give serious thought again to my original plans to continue my study for social work." Completing her bachelor's degree at age forty-six, she immediately entered a master's program in social work on a part-time basis, converting to full time a year later.

Another housewife, who had been editing some of her husband's work, decided to take some courses to increase her proficiency at that task. After she satisfactorily completed the courses, she applied for regular student status and received a scholarship which allowed her to attend full time. "From this time I had a definite wish to complete a full education and to prepare myself for a teaching career." She went on to complete the bachelor's degree at age forty-two, the master's degree at age forty-three, and immediately entered a Ph.D. program, all on a full-time basis.

The scholarly or intellectual life is, of course, an ideal for many. An immigrant from a Middle Eastern country reported that he entered graduate school at the age of thirty-seven because "scholarly pursuits, especially that of higher education, were nonexistent in [my country.] Coming to the United States afforded me a golden opportunity to pursue higher studies and develop my desire for scholarly work and attainment." He had formerly worked for American agencies in his native country after receiving a law degree. He received a master's degree in political science and a Ph.D. in history, and became an assistant and later associate professor of history in American colleges.

Again, the editor of a trade publication, who had formerly been an editor of an American Communist publication, said that the "chief reason for returning to college and taking a Ph.D. program was to return to intellectual life. . . . My education . . . had been very superficial and inadequate." His only degree was a B.S. in chemistry. He entered a Ph.D. program in international relations, specializing in Communist affairs. His return to school, he said, was "partly to use the best elements of [my] experience and partly to reeducate myself and find a place in the intellectual and political world on a new basis."

Scholarly interests were also evident in the case of a 57-year-old woman entering a Ph.D. program. She had returned to college part time to take some courses useful in her work as a free-lance writer and advertising consultant. Impressed by her writing and performance in school, several faculty members encouraged her to complete college. She began to consider becoming a college teacher of history but learned that she might face barriers in that field because of her age and sex. She turned to anthropology, where she had been told there were no such barriers. She is now completing her doctorate, having become an instructor in anthropology at age sixty-two.

An unusual case of an individual with intrinsic interest in a subject is an industrial engineer who was "fascinated with mass production and mass distribution." He returned to graduate school to combine two seemingly diverse disciplines as approaches to "social problems." As a management consultant, he had progressively shifted his speciality from mass production to new product design, marketing, and research. He also became a part-time lecturer in the behavioral sciences after he had developed unique and personal approaches to certain topics in psychology. Concerned with the problems of innovation, he entered graduate school at age thirty-nine to get a master's degree and Ph.D. in applied cultural anthropology. He later worked on advertising and product development as a cultural anthropologist in a research institute.

Similarly, a 40-year-old priest returned to school because he thought various psychological approaches could and should be given more attention in the training of parish priests and because he felt he "could make a contribution in this field that was much needed."

A woman working overseas as a project supervisor in a social service agency noted that she was increasingly involved in educational activities, which reawakened an earlier interest in teaching as a career. She already had a bachelor's degree in English and had studied toward a master's degree in American literature. At age forty-four she returned to graduate school to complete her master's degree. She then taught briefly while continuing work toward her Ph.D., but soon became a full-time student in modern British and American literature.

Quite different from the above examples, but still a case in which intrinsic interest stimulated a middle-aged person to return to graduate study, was the salesman who developed psychological difficulties following the death of his employer and the collapse of his employer's business. As a result, he received guidance and counseling for a period, during which he became interested in child development. He reentered college at age forty-three and received a bachelor's degree and later a master's degree in elementary education. He also took courses in administration, guidance, and counseling on a part-time and intermittent basis. Meanwhile, he worked as an elementary teacher, as a psychologist-counselor, and as a visiting professor of education.

The several marginal cases among those classified as having returned to school to satisfy "intrinsic" interest include a housewife who already had a bachelor's degree in philosophy and a master's in social science. She said, "I wanted to do something interesting and worthwhile which would also give me a measure of personal independence." She entered a master's program in library service. Another housewife said, "I should like to train myself for some concrete profession in which I could find personal and intellectual satisfaction, and by which, at the same time, I could earn some money." She entered an M.A. program at age fifty-three, completed it, and became a junior college instructor in English and American literature.

As Table 3.6 indicates, the primary reason that six of our seventy cases returned to professional or graduate school was to acquire new or increasingly important skills in their fields. An associate professor of economics, already holding a bachelor's and a master's degree in forestry and a Ph.D. in economics, became increasingly interested in mathematical economics. Convinced that this approach would dominate his discipline in the future, he first undertook part-time studies in mathematics, and at forty-one years of age entered a Ph.D. program in mathematics on a full-time basis. A staff development coordinator in a public health agency, who had a bachelor's degree in nursing education and a master's in public health nursing, noted the increasing need for mental health services and decided she "needed more formal preparation in this area." She had no need for an advanced degree, but enrolled in a Ph.D. program in psychology and mental health nursing in order to attend classes for a year. A Catholic parish priest who partially specialized in marriage counseling reported that "it became clear that many of the problems were emotional and mental instead of 'moral' problems." His earlier history had been quite varied: he had a B.S. and M.S. in chemistry, a graduate diploma in Anglican theology, service as an Anglican priest, and the necessary graduate study to become a Catholic priest. While continuing his parish duties, he enrolled in an M.A. and then a Ph.D. program in clinical psychology. His internship involved counseling alcoholics and he now hopes to become a psychologist or researcher in alcoholism.

Another priest, teaching philosophy in a high school, wanted "to keep abreast of the new trends and emphases" in philosophy and theology. He already held a bachelor's degree in French, a master's in philosophy, and a theology degree. He also wanted to write and teach at the college level. He obtained his Ph.D. in two years and is now on a college faculty, writing and publishing.

Two professors, neither of whom held the Ph.D., reported that they were attending school to keep up with the new materials and ideas in their field, to improve themselves, and to gain greater professionalism in their field. One was an associate professor of English with a master's degree in that field who enrolled in non-degree studies in a school of education. The second had bachelor's and master's degrees and had attended four summer institutes in mathematics. He entered a Ph.D. program in mathematics, but this may have been prompted by the usual reasons for seeking such a degree as much as it was to acquire newly emerging skills in the field, *per se*.

While many people indicated that returning to school satisfied earlier ambitions, only two said that this was the primary reason for their return, as Table 3.6 shows. One man who entered a Ph.D. program at the age of forty reported that "personally I never felt that it was a case of reentering graduate school. After receiving the B.S. degree I had set my mind on the graduate degree." He said that he had been prevented from finishing the degree by a series of personal and job difficulties. After acquiring his bachelor's degree in chemical engineering, he had gone to work because of "financial reasons." Some three years later, he set out to get a master's degree in the same field. It took him eight years. After still another eight years and at age forty, he returned to get his Ph.D. It took him five years of part-time and intermittent study and research.

The second case was a woman who had been unable to complete her Ph.D. studies when she was young because her earnings were essential to support her husband's graduate study. In the interim she taught in a high school and later kept house and raised their children. As she put it, "I *always intended* to return to school and earn my doctorate in order to return to college teaching." At age forty, as soon as her youngest child entered first grade, she started her Ph.D. study in American history and completed it in three years.

Although many noted that advanced study would improve their financial status, only two seemed to give it primacy. The first, an unmarried dentist with an extremely high income, enrolled at age thirty-eight in a full-time two-year master's program to prepare to become an orthodontist. He did it, he said, to improve his financial position. He expected his income to increase by at least one-third, conceivably to six figures. At the other extreme was a 37-year-old staff nurse in a public health agency, a graduate of a diploma school. "With . . . a husband of good potential but handicapped because of his race," she enrolled in a B.S. program to become a physical therapist, hoping to make a more secure future for herself and family, to increase her income, and to enter a field which would be less physically demanding in her old age.

A fairly large group was composed of persons who returned to advanced study to gain necessary credentials or skills in a field in which they were already involved. In these cases the respondents rarely mentioned the skills they would acquire in training but emphasized the credentials they would earn. Some of these respondents reported that the lack of a degree was all that was holding up their advancement. Some had even been employed in positions of the sort for which they were training, or could have easily obtained such positions, but felt that a complete set of credentials would be an advantage.

For example, a social worker with only a bachelor's degree in pre-social work had for some time acted as director of her agency. She had been told that the lack of a graduate degree would be the only reason she would not qualify for the position she was filling on a temporary basis. "I was personally responsible for the recruitment of the individual that was hired for this position," she said. She soon began full-time study in a master's program in social work at the age of forty-eight. Another case was that of a consulting psychotherapist and administrator in public and private agencies whose education included an undergraduate sociology major, a master's degree in social work, and certificates in psychoanalysis. He had been offered university teaching positions but decided that "having the Ph.D. would—in a variety of ways customary—give more freedom."

Slightly different was the warrant officer who was completing his part-time studies for a bachelor's degree in business administration. He became aware of "a long-standing desire to teach. On the basis of my experience I knew that I had the ability to teach, but I was informed that I needed a master's degree if I expected to teach at the college level." He therefore embarked upon the M.B.A. in a heavy part-time schedule. Meanwhile, he retired from the military and accepted a position as an assistant administrator and controller of a hospital. Upon completing the M.B.A. he realized that "a university instructor without a doctorate is virtually unpromotable." He is now slowly taking the education courses required for a public school teaching certificate.

One of the clearest statements of a desire for credentials, *per se,* was expressed by a high-school teacher of American history who had a bachelor's degree in chemistry and a master's in history. He said, "My primary reason for returning to graduate school was to obtain the seemingly required credentials which would permit me to gain access to positions of responsibility and power whereby I could be more effective in bringing about change in an educational system." Entering a Ph.D. program in educational administration at age thirty-seven, he has long-range ambitions to enter junior college administration and ultimately to become a college teacher.

In a similar situation, a research geophysicist with a bachelor's degree in geology came to feel "relatively uneducated. . . . I began to feel limits imposed by my previous education. . . . I noted others with no more ability but better education speed by. . . . I also realized that, although these same people couldn't match me in my own back yard, their breadth made them, for the most part, more valuable employees." After brushing up in mathematics and physics in part-time courses, he entered a full-time Ph.D. program in geophysics at age thirty-six. Similarly, a housewife with a bachelor's degree in music and a master's in early childhood education who had returned to work as a clinical assistant in psychology said that "after two years of work in that area it became clear that further opportunities would be very limited without an advanced degree." As a result, at thirty-nine she entered a Ph.D. program in psychology.

A housewife who was a registered nurse had returned for a public health nursing certificate at age thirty-four. After working for two years, she felt that she was "committed to this field." She further concluded: "To advance in this field, broader education is necessary, so I decided to work for a B.S. degree." She returned to school on a part-time basis at first, then completed the last year for her bachelor's degree as a full-time student. She then obtained a grant to get an M.Ed. in nursing, and now hopes to become a nursing instructor. Another example is a retired naval officer who is an assistant professor of management. His military experience and bachelor's and master's degrees in business helped him to get the job, but he concluded that "in order to be considered a qualified teacher the doctorate is becoming increasingly necessary . . . hence this course of action," i.e., entering a Ph.D. program in business at age thirty-nine.

A more unusual but similar instance was a vagabond artist who, during two years in a foreign country, began giving weekly lectures on contemporary art at a university. He began to write art criticism and his articles were published by a daily newspaper and then a weekly general circulation magazine. "The experience was exhilarating. . . . I felt I had a natural capacity for teaching but would be seriously hampered over the long haul without an education in depth. The lack of a teaching degree at that time did not interfere with my finding employment; however I felt that in the future a degree would be indispensable if I wished, as I do, to continue teaching." He returned to the United States and entered a bachelor's program in art education at age thirty-six.

As Table 3.6 indicates, approximately one-sixth of our cases reported their primary reason for returning to study as the availability of financial support. These cases do not include persons who wished to return to study for other reasons and who then obtained financial support. In five instances, financial support took the form of proffered or regular sabbatical leave or paid furlough. For instance, an elementary school teacher-in-charge with only a bachelor's degree in business said that "when the opportunity arose, placing before me the chance to obtain a degree in one year's time, I readily accepted it. It provided an opportunity to bring myself up to par with the new members of the teaching profession." On two days' notice she accepted a fellowship and sabbatical leave and entered a master's program in elementary education.

Similarly, an elementary school principal entered a doctoral program in education because "I was entitled to sabbatical leave." He was then forty-one and already held a bachelor's in elementary education and a master's in school administration. He added that "the salary schedule pays for graduate credit and I enjoy going to school." Again, a university administrator never found it practical to work for the Ph.D. degree until "I was granted a sabbatical from my post." He returned to a doctoral program at age thirty-six, "not only because I wanted to continue my education but I realized that I had progressed as far as I could in university administration without the Ph.D."

Two respondents were missionaries who utilized a furlough period to pursue educational interests. One, a Protestant missionary administrator in Europe, had already obtained bachelor's and master's degrees in European history and the B.D. in theology. He entered a Ph.D. program in church history. The other missionary had earlier received a bachelor's in education and the B.D. in theology. He returned on furlough from Asia and entered a master's program in linguistics, hoping to become a college teacher.

Several respondents returned to school primarily because their employers provided for it. A nun with a bachelor's degree in nutrition who was director of food service in her hospital said: "[I] had always been [interested] in the field of social work. The congregation to which I belong did not have any religious in that field." Her order decided it needed medical social workers and sent her, at age forty-seven to get a master's degree in social work. An administrator in a public welfare agency reported that she returned for an M.S.W. because stipends were available through federal and state funds. She had a variety of other reasons, including a desire to leave her present position because, she said, "I didn't think I would have the physical stamina to continue it indefinitely."

In another case, after a series of unsatisfying ventures in other fields, a young man in his thirties found a sense of personal accomplishment and commitment as a social worker in a welfare agency. He next became a youth worker in a children's institution, where he was later offered a traineeship. He took it because, he said, "I had nothing to lose," and entered a master's program in social work at age thirty-nine. Similarly, a language master at a preparatory school explained, "I was offered a huge scholarship in linguistics and accepted it." He originally had a bachelor's degree in comparative philology and classics and bachelor's and master's degrees in theology, but had become a language teacher because doctrinal differences made it impossible for him to teach in seminaries. At age thirty-eight he set out to earn a master's degree in linguistics and later entered a Ph.D. program.

Several other cases show how funds, available without any effort by the respondent, triggered a return to school. A technical consultant in a small contracting firm, who already had bachelor's and master's degrees in chemical engineering, never fulfilled a long-felt desire for more higher education. "When a friend of mine offered me a part of an N.S.F. grant to do my doctoral study . . . I accepted without hesitation." He was then thirty-seven years old. The most spontaneous of all was a woman who had operated a church basement kindergarten for nine years. She said, "I received a telephone call from a . . . professor asking if I would be interested in a scholarship. . . . I had been quite satisfied in my position . . . and had not considered seeking another degree." After hurried consideration of the situation, for she enjoyed an active family and social life, she entered an M.A. program in education.

While many of these older students relied heavily on the availability of fellowships or other financial support, several returned because of their own affluence or financial capacity. For instance, a jobber of imported goods reported, "I . . . remained engaged [in my business] until I felt that my investment was well protected by capable personnel and an established trade. Retaining only my financial interest in the business, I turned to the pursuit of my terminal degree and teaching." He had earned a business degree nearly two decades earlier, and he set out at age forty-two to get master's and doctoral degrees in business. He became an assistant professor of business.

Somewhat different was the German-born and educated man

who received a Ph.D. in economics and political science in 1935, but "[I] had to leave . . . academic life . . . in Germany because I am Jewish." Coming to the United States, he entered manufacturing and after two decades was president and general manager of his firm. At age forty-two he returned for an M.B.A. because he "was able to assemble enough funds while working in industry." He subsequently advanced from assistant to associate to full professor in business.

Affluence also affected an executive vice-president in marketing research. He had earlier obtained a degree in statistics and had done some graduate study in economics. From time to time he lectured in statistics at a graduate school of business. At age forty-two he found "an advantage" in leaving his job. He then noted, "I was in a position financially to support myself in school for a couple of years. [Because] graduate study was something I had always promised myself in some vague future plans . . . I decided to make it a fact." He started work on a Ph.D. in mathematics, planning to use it in a later return to business.

Another case was a man who, after acquiring an undergraduate degree in English, had advanced to a partnership in a highly specialized business firm. He then found himself "in a position where it was no longer necessary to work for a maximum salary." He shifted to other businesses which paid smaller salaries "while increasing the stimulus I derived from my work." History had long been one of his hobbies and then, he said, "It dawned on me that I enjoyed [history] a great deal more than any job I had held." At age forty-six he entered a master's program in American history and went on in pursuit of a Ph.D.

As in almost every classification, there were marginal cases here. Among those for whom financial capacity was the trigger was an older woman who had once attended college but had not been able to continue "due to financial difficulties . . . and many family problems. [When] financial strains had begun to ease," she completed her bachelor's degree in languages on a part-time basis. At fifty-eight, she entered a full-time master's program in German literature.

The second largest group of respondents were those whose primary motivation seemed to be that a change in the nature of their work was desirable or necessary. Seven—three men and four women—indicated considerable dissatisfaction with their former fields of work. One woman who had had clerical experience when she was young entered a bachelor's program in history at forty-five because "I was dissatisfied with the fields that were open to me with a limited educational background." After graduation she became a high-school teacher, but she soon became dissatisfied with that. At age fifty-one, she returned to get a master's in history, hoping to become a junior college teacher. Another, a 37-year-old working wife reported, "I decided to reenter . . . because there was no satisfaction nor room for improving oneself as a postal clerk." She entered a teacher's college for a B.S. in education and history.

Similarly, a government information officer with a degree in languages stressed his dissatisfaction with publicity as a field, his own performance in it, and the bureaucratic nature of the large organizations in which he worked. He therefore got a master's in political science and continued studying for a Ph.D., meanwhile working as an assistant professor and researcher in the same field.

A 48-year-old assistant sales manager with a B.A. had long been dissatisfied with his job, but, he said, "As the years went on, I became convinced that I could not afford to switch careers. I was afraid to. [After being elected to a local library board], I became interested in libraries . . . and from time to time I toyed with the idea of going to library school at night." His decision to return became definite when he learned that he could get the necessary financial aid to complete a master's program in library science.

Another example concerns a free-lance writer who had worked in various aspects of television, marketing, and sales. His reason for returning to school: "Basic dissatisfaction with the direction in which my career had evolved . . . I felt I must make a radical shift back toward areas and roles corresponding to [my] basic interests and values or I would . . . feel I had misspent my energies." With a bachelor's degree in social science and graduate study in urban land economics, this 48-year-old man entered a Ph.D. program in political science.

An editor of religious publications with a bachelor's degree in history and a master's in religious education reported that she "became dissatisfied with editorial work and the daily routine of office schedules and the lack of contact with people." College life offered her the exposure to people which she desired. She entered teaching, obtained a master's in history, and went on for the Ph.D.

A woman who graduated from college with a degree in English during the depression held a series of jobs as an executive secretary and administrative worker in unions and private business. She decided to enter graduate school because "the administrative work I had performed for some twenty-three years no longer held any challenge for me." She obtained an M.A. in English in two years of part-time study while working, and then the Ph.D. in four years. She has since become a college teacher.

We have discussed lack of promotability as a reason to return to school to gain the necessary skills or credentials. Others faced with job difficulties moved off into new directions. For instance, a sales representative decided it was necessary to look for a new field because of "a change in my job circumstance." A better job which he had hoped to get was clearly going to be given to a relative of the boss who had just been brought into the firm. Also, as this respondent indicated, "I had lost much of my enthusiasm for the job." Continuing as a salesman, he got a master's degree in anthropology by studying part time. He then began full-time study for the Ph.D. Another example is an accounting clerk who grew increasingly uneasy about her job as a result of several mergers and increased use of electronic data-processing equipment. She concluded that "the position I held would gradually be changed to demanding only routine tasks. . . . I had a need to remain in closer contact with people." Thus, at thirty-six, she began part-time study while working, left her job for full-time study at thirty-eight, and earned a bachelor's degree in psychology at forty. She continued on for a master's in social work.

In other cases, the desire to change was real, though not as tinged with dissatisfaction or fear. For instance, a nursery school director with a B.S. in psychology felt her age "a limiting factor" in her work, and "I wanted to prepare myself for some other aspect of early childhood education. . . . Another factor . . . was my desire to work with the 'disadvantaged' child and the realization that I needed further knowledge to do so." At age forty-two she returned for a master's in early childhood education and later became the leader of a teaching team in a Head Start program. Another woman with a bachelor's in pre-social work and a master's in elementary education reported, "I had been teaching third grade for twelve years. I felt that some sort of change would be desirable. My district offered a liberal sabbatical policy. I could not travel . . . so I decided to take a year to study." She entered a special study program to become a guidance counselor.

Another among those for whom a change was necessary was the naval officer approaching mandatory retirement at age forty-nine. He had a B.S. in electrical engineering and a law degree but had not made up his mind about a post-retirement career. Meanwhile, his wife was taking an introductory course in library science at a local junior college. Through family discussions, his interest was aroused and he took the same course. "I decided that librarian was to be my new profession and that that profession needed me." Upon retirement, he obtained a master's in library science, became a college reference librarian, and later was appointed an assistant law librarian in a university.

Some who felt a need for change had had interesting and successful careers. A chemical engineer with advanced study in his field had moved up to executive positions and was ready to enter company headquarters. At that point, he decided to get a Ph.D. in business and enter university life. He said, "I made the decision only after long and careful consideration. . . . I no longer felt that being an executive officer of a large corporation in [a major city] represented what I really wanted out of life." A self-employed interior designer decided, "I would like to move in a new direction, to put my experience and competence to work in a service area." At fifty, she earned a bachelor's degree in sociology after four years of part-time study. At fifty-two, she entered a master's program in educational administration and then studied an additional year for a professional diploma. Finally she entered governmental service as a personnel administrator in the poverty program.

Several responses were somewhat distinctive and difficult to classify. One man had alternated periods of study in a school for actors, a navigation school, a bachelor's degree program in cultural anthropology, and a postgraduate year of South Asian area studies with periods of employment as an actor, military officer, and public information official overseas. He then tried for three years to become a writer, but "it did not work out." Wanting a "way out" he switched to become a cameraman apprentice and later a journeyman, for he wanted "employment requiring all my energies, mental and physical, and no personal thoughts whatever." After three years, he decided that "life had become deadly dull." At age forty-six he entered a master's program in a non-Western language because of "the desire to find . . . areas of experience as removed from my own as possible."

Another distinctive response came from a 42-year-old housewife with a retarded child requiring institutionalization and a husband whom she described as "unsettled in work, unrealistic, . . . dependent." She had earlier received a degree in sociology, studied in a leading secretarial school, been a lieutenant during World War II, studied interior decorating and law, and worked as a secretary. She reported that "[I] knew I could achieve satisfactions from returning to school and making my future more secure both financially and 'coming alive' again." She completed an M.A. program in education, taught for a year and a half in a junior high school, and returned to a doctoral program in educational psychology, at first on a part-time and later on a full-time basis.

Another unusual response came from a former director of admissions at a women's college who had bachelor's and master's degrees in botany and graduate study in education. Pressures mounted in her work. She decided to enter a school library service because "it would make possible more flexible and perhaps less demanding jobs and part-time work in any community when I reached retirement age." In a similar vein, a 53-year-old woman decided to use a small sum of money left by her father to pay for "training which could be used in any part of the country in which my husband and I might settle after his retirement which he wanted to plan for early." She earned a master's in library service and worked briefly as an assistant librarian. However, her husband decided to travel and she had not worked for five years at the time of her response.

There was only one individual in our group who returned to school for avocational reasons. He was a successful dentist who had been widowed and remarried. He spent a good deal of time in volunteer work at hospitals and institutions for children. He explained that his own children and his step-children of his second marriage had all grown up. While continuing his practice, he entered a master's program in education at age fifty-eight on a heavy part-time schedule because "I just want to teach the underprivileged child—the one that was neglected like I was when I was a child. That's all."

Another way to look at this group is in terms of the type of career shift respondents made or were making by returning to school. As Table 3.7 indicates, half of the respondents were entering or moving upward within a professional field, while the other half were shifting among closely related fields, making a major reorientation within a field, or making a major change in occupation.

Most of the fifteen who were entering or preparing to enter a professional occupation for the first time were women. Five of the eleven women had been housewives and four had been clerical workers. One man had been a salesman. The remainder might be classified as marginal professionals, including two free-lance writers, a "political analyst" from another country who had been temporarily employed in the United States as a tailor, a field interviewer, and a cameraman who had formerly been a public relations officer.

TABLE 3.7. *Types of Occupational Mobility Sought through a Return to Professional or Graduate School, by Sex*

	Men	*Women*	*Total*
Entering a profession	4	11	15
Upward within a profession	11	9	20
Shift between closely related fields or within a broad field	14	4	18
Major change in occupation	11	6	17
Total	40	30	70

Nearly all of the twenty moving upward within a professional field were making what could be considered normal upward movements toward new or increased administrative responsibility or toward a greater degree of specialization within a field. This group was comprised of proportionate numbers of men and women. Ten were in education and three were in social work. The remainder were in geophysics, chemical engineering, dentistry, psychology, church work, and nursing. In all of these cases, of course, the added education might later permit a major shift in function, particularly to teaching in their fields, but that was not the obvious intent of the added education.

The two remaining groups, who were shifting fields in some sense or other, were largely made up of men. Those who were making shifts between related fields or within a general field have been characterized earlier as making a "45° turn," because they continue to rely heavily on their previously acquired skills, but they

nevertheless are making a significant shift in occupation or function. Five businessmen and two military officers wanted to become
professors of business or economics and three secondary school
teachers wanted to become college teachers in their fields. Four
others were involved in a complex efforts to expand or introduce
psychology into various service programs. An economist and a
market researcher were seeking mathematics degrees to enable them
to make a significant change in the nature of their functions within
their original fields. Others making a major shift within a general
field included an artist who was becoming an art teacher, a nurse
who was becoming a physical therapist, and a schoolteacher who
was becoming a guidance counselor. In addition, an engineer-buyer
was becoming a lawyer but intended to remain within the buying
function.

The final group consisted of those who were making more dras-
tic occupational changes. It is important to note that there was
considerable overlap between their former and their new fields. In
one sense, the difference between them and the third group above
is merely one of degree. But if the one group is characterized as
taking a "45° turn," this last group was taking a "90° turn." Thus,
their shift is essentially a sideways movement, i.e., a clear-cut
change in career fields. The transitions in this group were quite diverse: a social service supervisor to English literature, two editors
to the study of international relations and history, a parish priest
to clinical psychology, a missionary to linguistics, a hospital nu-
tritionist to medical social work, an interior designer to educational
administration, a sales representative to anthropology, an information officer to political science, a dentist to elementary teaching,
and three others—a sales manager, an educational administrator, and
an engineering naval officer—to librarianship.

Several interesting relationships between the type of career
change and expressed reason for returning to school can be seen.
As Table 3.8 indicates, the large majority of those who were entering a profession for the first time and those who were making a

TABLE 3.8. *Primary Reasons for Entering or Reentering Professional or Graduate School, by Type of Career Change*

	Type of Career Change			
Reason for Study	Entering a profession	Upward within a profession	Shift within a field or to related field	Major change
Intrinsic interest in subject or field	6	2	3	5
To acquire new or increasingly important skills in field	—	2	3	1
To realize an earlier ambition	—	1	1	—
To improve financial status	—	1	1	—
To gain necessary credentials or skills	—	5	4	—
Available support, funds, fellowships, etc.	—	8	2	1
Affluence or financial capacity	1	—	2	2
Change desirable or necessary	5	1	2	6
Other	3	—	—	2
Total	15	20	18	17

major shift in their occupation or function were doing so either because they had a high intrinsic interest in the subject or field or because a change in their field or function appeared desirable or necessary. The converse was also true, for the large majority of both those who returned to school because of high intrinsic interest in a subject or field and those who returned because a change in their situation was desirable or necessary were either entering a profession for the first time or were making a major shift in their occupation or function at the professional level.

There is another instance of a close relationship between the type of career change and the reasons for returning to school. Nearly all of those who returned primarily because support, funds, or the like were available were moving up within a profession, and they comprised nearly half of those moving up in this fashion. A significant number of those moving up within a profession had returned to school to acquire necessary credentials or skills in fields in which they were already involved. However, many of those who had returned to school to acquire credentials were making a major reorientation within a general field. Each of these was becoming a teacher in a field in which he considered himself already competent, but returned to gain the credentials and perhaps some skills. These included two military officers who wanted to teach business management, an artist becoming an art teacher, and a psychologist preparing for a university teaching post.

There were no other instances of close relationships. The striking point about the eighteen persons who were shifting from one field to a related field or who were making a major reorientation within a general field is that they exhibited a diverse set of reasons for returning to school, with no reason or set of reasons dominating the group.

The main point which emerges from this panorama is the wide range of specific motives which led these respondents to enter or reenter professional or graduate school as full-time or nearly full-time students at an age definitely beyond the conventional school years. There does not seem to be a "typical" older student. A second major conclusion is that the primary reasons for returning to school were overwhelmingly positive. Very few made the shift because of general or particular dissatisfaction with their previous situation. On the whole, there is little evidence that those who returned were "unstable." While they are an adventurous lot, few seemed to be "unconventional." A significant number returned for mixed or mundane reasons. This seems to characterize the many classified here as returning to acquire necessary credentials or because financial support was available. Even in these groups, however, some returned to school for more positive reasons. The most positive motivation was found among the relatively high number who returned to school because of their high order of interest in a particular subject or field, because they wanted to acquire new skills in their fields, or because they had achieved personal affluence and were thus able to seek out newer, more personally rewarding careers.

4. Opportunities and Barriers

WHETHER MIDDLE-AGED PERSONS are able to enter a new profession or substantially change their level or type of position within a field depends directly on the availability of the necessary educational programs and the success of these adults in obtaining admission. A second factor may be the availability of financial aid in particular fields and the extent to which middle-aged students may be able to obtain support.

To get information on these and other aspects of the attendance at professional and graduate schools of middle-aged students, we interviewed some sixty university officials, including presidents, vice-presidents, deans, directors, associate and assistant deans, admissions officers, placement officers, financial aid officers, etc. The interviews were based on a relatively simple open-ended questionnaire which functioned as an extended agenda for discussion. Interviews rather than formal questionnaires were used to avoid forcing the respondents into *a priori* responses. We suspected, and it turned out, that the nuances of the situation were often more important than any particular succinct statement that could be developed.

We interviewed at least one and usually several officials from nearly all institutions offering graduate and professional training in our four metropolitan areas. In any sizable metropolitan area there are usually at least two universities, perhaps of differing rank, as well as a variety of relatively small professional schools. In each area, we visited several persons in each of the major institutions—"major institution" defined in terms of the number of students enrolled in or degrees granted per year by its professional or graduate programs and schools. We excluded all liberal arts colleges, and

54

most small independent professional schools, such as those devoted to law, music, optometry, and the like. However, of the independent institutions, we included two teachers' colleges, one school of pharmacy, one seminary and two technical institutes. With the exception of the teachers' colleges, none of these independent institutions had a significant number of older students.

We decided to canvass various institutions in each metropolitan area because we felt that different institutions in an area might have different, but complementary, policies with respect to the admission of older applicants. A person who might not want to attend or who might not be admitted at one institution might be accepted at another. Institutions often specialize and are stronger in some departments and schools than others. They also tend to serve certain population groups—in terms of general level of ability, socioeconomic status, race, religion, sex, and the like. We speculated that older students might have to go to some lengths to find an institution or department which would admit them, and would therefore be found least often in leading universities. We had to qualify these expectations when we found that a middle-aged person tends to apply to only one institution.

However, a metropolitan area turned out to be a significant delineator of the options of middle-aged persons in a quite different way. By and large, metropolitan universities serve commuting students, whereas rural universities serve students who move to the campus. Because of ties to family, home, job, etc., middle-aged students are usually commuters. Only in metropolitan areas can there be a significant number of qualified middle-aged persons who desire to attend professional or graduate school.

ADMISSION POLICIES

We found that in most universities information about admissions and the experiences of older persons cannot be obtained by interviewing those in central administration. The admissions process is usually heavily decentralized, and the criteria for admission are often not clear. Each person involved in the admissions process tends to impose his own perhaps idiosyncratic standards. Deans of graduate schools often have one view of the admissions process and standards, and departmental chairmen and assistant deans for admissions have another.

The locus of decision-making and power in the admissions process is different in different institutions. In some cases, admissions is the function of departmental chairmen and in others there may be a faculty admissions committee. In some departments, professors pass on those who hope to study in their area of specialization.

Some deans of graduate schools have little more than a clerical function; their offices collect the documents required of applicants and send each completed set to the appropriate department, where a decision is made independently. In other universities, the graduate dean may closely supervise the various departments and impose more or less standard policies. In most universities, admissions are handled independently by the graduate schools and the respective professional schools. A few universities have a central director of admissions who attempts, with varying degrees of success, to achieve some consistency with respect to the admissions policies of the various schools and divisions.

Almost every university has some kind of formal or informal policy stance with respect to its educational mission, which may range from that of a service center for the community to that of a center of excellence. Whatever the central ideological or policy stance, it is not uncommon for various groups, departments, or schools within a university rather openly to take stances which are at variance with the purported university policy. A department to which many more able students apply that it can possibly admit may be relatively free to develop its own policies, while one which has difficulty in recruiting an adequate number of students may also have a policy different from the basic university policy. A department or school that produces a "profit" which helps support or subsidize other less popular or more expensive departments may be free to follow its own tendencies. A department or school may have an admission policy different from university policy if it enjoys strong support from important groups such as influential alumni, public officials, and the like.

As a result, admissions policies within universities are quite uneven. Applications from older persons may be viewed favorably in some departments and unfavorably in others. The policy in individual departments may change from year to year as different members of the faculty serve as chairman or members of the admissions committee.

Since many people are usually involved in the admissions decision, applicants who satisfy everyone in the admissions process are admitted. This often means that each person in the process has a potential veto, or "blackball." Sometimes a vetoed applicant may have his case reopened if he is strongly supported. Still, if anyone in the process has a bias of any sort against older persons, whether he is conscious of it or not, it is likely that older persons will be rejected.

Secretarial personnel often play a crucial role in the detailed operation of departments and schools. Many are highly competent, but in some cases we noted extremely personal approaches to admissions by secretarial personnel. The chances are that this adversely affects a higher proportion of older applicants.

Finally, higher education is in a state of ferment and is rapidly growing at present, with a resultant high degree of mobility manifested by professors and administrators. The majority of people above the level of permanent secretary or administrative assistant whom we interviewed had been in these positions for less than two years. Indeed, almost every person interviewed started with a disclaimer that he had entered his position so recently that he could not tell us about present policy and would rather speak about the policies which prevailed in his previous job. Nevertheless we believe that the information in the aggregate presents an accurate picture.

The net result of all of these factors was that we usually did not get a simple straightforward response to our inquiry about a school's or department's policy with respect to the admission of persons aged thirty-five and over. We encountered only one university with a hard and fast rule against the admission of anyone past age thirty-five. We ran into a significant number of situations, particularly in the natural and physical sciences and engineering, where an application for full-time study by a person past age thirty-five came up so infrequently that it presented no real issue.

We can divide the institutions, schools, or departments into two major classifications: 1) those in which age itself plays no role in the admissions process, although factors associated with age may have a bearing; 2) those where age itself plays a role and is specifically taken into account by admissions officers. The reasons for taking age into account are quite diverse and will be discussed subsequently.

Wherever age is taken into account, however, we found a broad range in the ages which the institution or the admitting officer considers relevant. Almost no institution considers the age of a person still in his twenties a negative factor. Some institutions, however, raise questions about applicants older than thirty. Some admissions officers tend to define older students as those between thirty and forty, since they have so few above forty. Others tend to define older students as those above forty; still others referred to those above forty-five, believing that the age of younger persons presented no significant issue. Some began to consider the age factor as special only after age fifty-five and a few made—or said they made—no distinctions unless the candidate was sixty or older.

Although most universities, colleges, and graduate schools deal differently with older applicants, we found that few had official policies with respect to age. No more than a handful had an explicit statement in their catalogs with respect to age. One university, as noted, openly sets an absolute age limit of thirty-five for admission. Its officials justify this policy on the grounds that older students have ample opportunities in other nearby institutions. One school stated that it imposes no arbitrary age limits, but warns in its catalog that age may be a handicap in gaining a job.

Indeed, a few universities tend to encourage or prefer older students. This is common in institutions which have actively supported continuing education programs. These institutions and programs tend to have more part-time than full-time students. In some institutions, the regular departments and divisions sometimes resist the continuing education program and often resist admitting older students. At others, the regular departments recommend that older applicants apply to the continuing education divisions. Sometimes this is simply to avoid older applicants on the assumption that they are not serious candidates for graduate degrees. Other regular departments may send older applicants to continuing education programs to test their interest, to help them reestablish evidence of ability, and to update their skills. Of course, older applicants sometimes resent this or any other practice which suggests that the regular departments do not consider them serious applicants.

Some graduate schools and departments feel a responsibility toward their own former students who return to complete or continue their work, even after many years. Acceptance of a middle-aged former student may be more or less *pro forma*, and he or she may even receive full credit for prior work. Re-admission is sometimes encouraged in that such applications are handled directly through the departments while first admissions are handled through admissions offices. On the other hand, some schools may give former students no credit for earlier work. Predictably, they have relatively few former students. There seems to be no particular relationship between the quality of the school and its policy with respect to the re-admission of former students or the granting of credit for prior work.

Faculty wives often find it easy to be accepted, even if they are over thirty-five, when they apply to their husband's or a neighboring institution. They may not be particularly welcome, but deans and chairmen hesitate to reject the wife of a colleague.

An admissions officer may react differently to older applicants, depending on the program they seek to enter. In many cases, no questions are raised about an application to a master's program but doubts may be raised with respect to older applicants to a Ph.D. program. This may be due to a variety of factors, including the length and rigor of the program. Some graduate departments are primarily interested in Ph.D. candidates; other departments have many students who plan to be or who are high-school teachers. It is usually more difficult for an older applicant to enter the former than the latter, even if he intends to get a Ph.D. This may be due to the fact that departments which stress the Ph.D. are usually stronger. Even a strong department will be more willing to accept the older applicant if it has a master's program which can be used as a try-out period.

A crucial factor in the attitude of graduate schools and departments with respect to the admission of older candidates is the relative availability of resources. Institutions with limited funds can admit only a limited number of students and they often tend to admit few older applicants. Some may have an arbitrary rule; others may have no interest in expanding their programs and therefore no interest in taking on unconventional students. Schools with limited resources quite often find it administratively simpler to ignore unusual applications or to process them less assiduously. Schools with limited resources may also restrict their scope in one way or another, such as avoiding service functions and concentrating on the quality of their student body, or by specializing only in certain types of courses or students. The pressure of scarce resources on the type of program and the general availability of opportunities for older candidates seems more prevalent in private institutions. However, some public institutions have real budgetary difficulties, are not expanding, and simply are not interested in applicants who are in any way out of the ordinary.

The majority of universities and schools seem to have policies which directly restrict opportunities for older applicants even though they do not make a formal statement to that effect. Some have a deliberately consciously negative attitude toward the older person; others are simply more positively oriented toward the younger applicant. Some say that they have doubts about older students. As one graduate dean put it, "Graduate study . . . is made available primarily to younger people. . . . Our graduate program . . . does recognize the possibility of older, serious students . . . but in all fairness to them, it reviews their plans with even greater care to make certain that they are feasible." Another stated that the "applicant over thirty-five is treated as a special case. We make sure the applicant understands that as a new Ph.D. . . . he will be starting professionally where men at least ten years his junior normally start and that many colleges and universities (particularly small ones) are often reluctant to hire instructors or beginning assistant professors over thirty-five. We are also especially careful in checking the applicant's academic qualifications. Has he been away from academic work so long that he has formed an unrealistic idea of Ph.D. requirements? Does he think that a dissertation topic would be acceptable today because it might have been so twenty years ago? Does he realize fully the time he will have to spend on his degree? Is he aware of the cost and can he afford it?"

One dean said that his school has a policy of actively discouraging older students by deliberately raising a series of questions about their age, length of time out of school, ability to study and spend long hours at it, the great changes which have transpired in their field, etc. Another dean spoke of the great deal of "negative counseling" he did with older applicants.

One common approach to an older applicant is to ask how many years of productive capacity he can contribute after getting the degree, if he enters the program late in life. This is particularly true in Ph.D. programs, which are lengthy and expensive in various ways. The decision to admit a person is an investment decision, and an economic calculus may be used in the light of the scarce resources for education. The calculus may be expressed in terms of the allocation of a limited number of openings, the utilization of public funds, the utilization of university funds, the utilization of faculty time, or the like. Admitting officers often feel a responsibility consciously to compare investment returns. Some believe that they are making an investment for society; they assert that they must ask questions about the relative social rate of return for a given investment. For others the criterion is expressed in terms of the responsibility of their graduate school to staff the universities of the nation. In this calculus, an investment in a student aged forty is likely to produce only half the future university faculty time as an investment in a student aged twenty-two.

At the departmental level, the responsibility to make socially wise investments is often expressed in terms of the likelihood of significant future contributions to the field. In addition, some officers are even conscious of whether older or younger students are more likely to support the institution by donations or in the legislature. In the one university which limited its responsibility to the education of the young, this policy was justified on the grounds of relatively limited resources and inability to spread these resources over a great many different functions.

Many admissions officers argue the economic calculus from a different point of view. They seem to see themselves in *loco parentis* to the older applicant. As one dean stated it: "The doctorate is expensive in time and money, including the lost income while in school. With only ten to fifteen years of service after the doctorate, there is no opportunity to get a return on the investment. A person past forty-five should take various types of continuing education. The doctorate may not be of great value to him, to his colleagues, or to his students." The theme that denying or discouraging the older applicant was in his best interest took many other forms, but it recurred repeatedly.

It should be noted, however, that one dean in a school of social work took a different stance on the "return on investment" argument. Because of the high attrition rates among young women after they begin work, he said, the expected work life in the field may be greater for a middle-aged than for a younger student.

There is a subtle distinction between those who state that they consciously deal differently with older students because of some investment criterion and those who feel that older applicants may have more shortcomings than younger applicants. One admissions official said, for instance, that we "think more carefully" about older students. Another said that older applicants tend to be "guilty unless proven innocent" of a variety of shortcomings.

The key problem seems to be that of assessing older persons and their likelihood of success in graduate programs. The difficulties in assessing older persons tend to turn on two kinds of questions: first, the reasons they are returning to school; and second, difficulties in assessing their academic qualities.

Many admissions officers confess to being concerned about the basic reason that an applicant tries to reenter school at a later age than usual. The reason for reentering is seen as a strong clue to the probabilities of completion as well as having some bearing on the function of the school. For instance, if an applicant has failed at his previous line of work, most schools would be extremely reluctant to admit him. On the other hand, if the previous work was stultifying, and particularly if it involved a conflict between competitive and noncompetitive values, many schools may be more favorably inclined. Of course, if an older applicant has been a success and now states that his interests are changing, there may be little resistance to him.

Many schools try to avoid the older applicant who seems to have only a "bookish" interest or who thinks "school is a good idea." The former attitude is quite common among applicants to such departments as English, psychology, sociology, anthropolgy, etc., while the latter is widespread and encountered even by schools of business. On the other hand, if the applicant indicates "evidence of a major commitment to intellectual life," he may very well be accepted. Of course, some admissions officers seem to doubt that older persons, and particularly women, can be seriously interested in intellectual affairs. Others, however, believe that both the old and the young can be cultivated or inducted into an intellectual attitude.

One other concern of admissions officers is the reality of the expectations which the older applicant holds. If his expectations seem realistic and attainable, he is more likely to be accepted. Finally, if an older applicant is performing well in his occupation but wants to overcome deficiencies in either basic skills or general education, admissions officers tend to look at him more favorably.

Sometimes older applicants are deliberately discouraged in order to test how sincere their interests are. In these cases, persistence often wins out, either because the admissions officer cannot resist forever or because he interprets persistence as a sign of basic interest. Indeed, the admissions officer may reluctantly conclude that anyone who really wants to do something has the right to do it, even if it is a mistake.

The assessment of quality also raises some questions with respect to older applicants. They often find it difficult to obtain academic references. Admission depends to a varying extent on letters of recommendation from undergraduate professors. If one has been out of school for ten to fifteen years, such letters are not only hard to get but may even be irrelevant. Second, other references may or may not be useful. If a person has been employed outside the field in which he wants to go back to school, letters of recommendation from employers have relatively little meaning. Indeed, the fact that a person has been successful in employment does not necessarily indicate probable success in an academic discipline. Third, test scores may not have the same meaning for older and younger students. Youngsters are more attuned to taking tests and may score better. On the other hand, there is considerable skepticism about the meaning of the tests for students of any age. Indeed, admissions officers sometimes use test scores to justify admission or rejection of an applicant when the decision to admit or reject was based on other, less precise criteria. Low scores can be used to reject an older person when he might have been accepted if he had been younger. Fourth, it is difficult to appraise the adequacy of an older person's background. The content of various academic fields is changing rapidly. A bachelor's degree obtained ten to fifteen years ago is not the equivalent of one obtained recently, whether in science, sociology, literature, or any other field. Changes occur not only in the content of a field but also in theoretical systems, topics of interest, tools, definitions, and other aspects of particular disciplines. As a result, older persons are considered to be handicapped in fitting into a field, no matter how good their original background. This issue does not arise for those older applicants who recently have been in school completing or updating their undergraduate education.

On the other hand, intervening activities may be revealing and useful in appraising the quality of an older person. If one has been in teaching, research, or similar work, his interim activities may be favorable, for the transition to the academic world may not be so difficult. Indeed some admissions officers try to be circumspect in appraising an older person with some flecks in his history. They know that simply because he has lived longer, an older person may have one or more mistakes on his record. They do not feel that older and younger people can be compared according to the same terms. Young people write essays which suggest all their bright hopes for the future and which explain away some of their mistakes. With older persons, reality is much more evident and cannot be rationalized or explained away. This tends to introduce a possible bias against the older person, which some admissions officers try to guard against.

In general, it seems that the older the applicant, the higher his qualifications must be to gain admission. One admissions officer suggested, for instance, that applicants over fifty have to be "very superior" to be admitted. Another said that every student is a risk; well-qualified people are always admitted whether they are young or old. With high risk or marginal candidates, however, he said, "I always favor the young." He also pointed out that the risk is even greater in the case of an older person whose background greatly differs from the field he wants to enter.

There are other tendencies which militate against the older applicant even when there is no policy or bias against age, *per se.* One graduate school, for instance, favors candidates who have completed their undergraduate education within the past five years. This works to the detriment of older students out of school for some time, although it has no bearing on the older person who has recently completed an undergraduate program and wants to enter graduate study. The earlier noted tendency in some schools to refuse credits for courses taken years earlier operates in a similar fashion.

Some leading institutions have eliminated or seek to eliminate part-time students and night and Saturday classes. Older students, particularly women, are a higher proportion of students in those classes. Consequently the elimination of such classes makes it more difficult for older persons to test their capacity, reestablish credentials, acquire references, and update skills prior to full-time study.

Many schools are attempting to be more selective in admissions in order to raise the quality of their student bodies or reduce the proportion who fail to complete the program. With a tightening of standards and more competitive admissions, older applicants are more likely to be eliminated.

Some schools actively recruit, but only among the young. With a few notable exceptions, graduate and professional schools do not seem to want it known that they have many older students. Some professional schools, such as those of education, social work, or library service are exceptions and do recruit older applicants. These schools nevertheless seek to maintain the image of a young, vibrant, dynamic institution. Unless specific inquiry is made, their high proportion of middle-aged students is not evident.

The question of overt, covert, or indirect resistence to older applicants is largely irrelevant in a great many departments and schools, precisely because they rarely encounter older applicants. This is particularly true in the natural and physical sciences, engineering, and mathematics. Occasionally an older person will apply for entry to graduate study in an applied science field, especially newer fields in which the manpower demands are great, the content has changed drastically, and financial support is available. Examples of these fields have included meteorology, oceanography, and the space sciences.

In some schools age seems to be totally irrelevant. No records are kept about the age of students, even on personal record forms. One could guess the approximate age of an applicant by the date he graduated from high school, but the school is clearly not interested in age, *per se.*

These schools which have open policies with respect to older students assert that they make no formal or informal distinctions among applicants on the basis of age. One must take their assertions as true in intent, although not necessarily true in fact. It was not uncommon to find on further probing that open policies are often contradicted in fact unless there was, and sometimes in spite of, a conscious effort to implement the policy.

Certain universities have a basically liberal stance on all admissions and have few formal requirements although they seek high quality. This stance is characteristic of a strong liberal arts or humanities orientation. One dean said, "We have had too much experience with 'inadmissibles' who later came on well." Such institutions often admit a good many "questionable" students, even though many drop out later. Although some think this is a frivolous policy, those who follow it think of it as "democratic." Another dean said, "In the graduate school we do not see ourselves as educators of the young. . . . Rather we are a community of scholars. You can join us if you are able to contribute." One dean related this open stance to the school's "populist tradition." Another, a dean at a Jesuit university, related his school's open policy to the fact that the order's founder, St. Ignatius Loyola, had shifted in middle age from the military to the priesthood and the education of the young.

Religiously oriented schools often maintain an open stance with respect to those connected with their community, because the school's main purpose is to serve their religion and its institutions. Catholic universities, for instance, regularly accept middle-aged religious and lay employees of Catholic social service agencies, parochial schools, and the like. In many such cases, the only question is whether the applicant's superior wants him or her to obtain the added education. One dean in a secular school of pharmacy in a hospital complex reported that he had admitted a 63-year-old nun to become a pharmacist, simply because the Mother Superior of a neighboring hospital had asked him to do so; he did not raise a single question when she called.

There have also been a sprinkling of special programs established for older applicants. Some city boards of education have organized special programs to attract former teachers or college graduates into teaching. Some of these programs are relatively abbreviated, but others run for considerable time and involve a significant acquisition of skills. The National Association of Social Workers has actively promoted a second careers program clearly directed at people who have been in other fields and middle-aged women returning to the labor force. The School of General Studies at Columbia University, with Ford Foundation support, operated a New Careers program to help persons enter professional service fields, often starting with undergraduate education. Finally, several graduate schools of business or management run special master's degree programs for those between the ages of about thirty and forty who are nominated and supported by their employers.

In some programs significant numbers of older students have long been common. For example, at one time nearly all Ed.D. candidates had had extensive administrative experience. We encountered one program leading to a doctor of sacred theology which was the final step after four years in a bachelor of arts program and four years in the bachelor of divinity program. However, admission to the doctoral program is not even considered until after several years in pastoral or teaching duty subsequent to the B.D. degree. With such a long period of study, work, and research, most students do not finish this program until well past thirty-five.

With increasing emphasis on and support for graduate education, however, these patterns seem to be phasing out. Increasingly, Ed.D. programs are being designed for those who have just finished their collegiate education, perhaps with a period of internship as an explicit part of the educational experience. Similarly, the prolonged, drawnout pursuit of the Ph.D. and other doctoral degrees is under increasing disfavor. Students are receiving financial support from government, foundations, and the schools themselves, in order to shorten the time it takes to get the degree.

Finally, despite strong indications that older applicants were being resisted in particular universities, we often found there were a great many more older students than university officials thought. Whether the resistances are a response to the large number of applicants, or whether the applicants are more persistent than admissions officers are resistant, is not clear. On the other hand, schools which espoused completely open admissions policies were often found to have few older students. A disconcertingly large number of officials at universities were uninterested in why they had so few older applicants when their official policy was an open one. Whenever we could probe, we usually found some of the factors cited above, such as particular departments or individuals in the admissions process contradicting the stated policy or because other policies tended to eliminate older applicants.

Admissions officers could provide us with little data bearing on their older applicants. A few pieces of data suggest that in general the proportion of applicants at a given school who are accepted by it decreases with age. Some data suggest that the acceptance rates of those in their early thirties is lower than of those in their twenties, but that acceptance rates for those in the late thirties are higher. At these schools, acceptance rates of those in the middle forties decline again. It may be that those who are seeking admission in their early thirties have been unsuccessful in employment and are trying to reorient their lives, while those who return in their late thirties or early forties are a more purposeful and able group.

The data also suggest that of all those who are accepted by a school, a much higher proportion of the older students actually enter. Older students usually apply to only one institution and, if they are admitted, almost surely enter that institution. Younger applicants tend to apply to several institutions; if they are accepted at more than one—as many are—they must perforce turn down the extra acceptances. Because the data are from institutions and not from the applicants, it is not entirely clear that the proportion of all who apply at one or more schools and in fact do enter a school is higher among the young than older applicants, but this is probably true.

FINANCIAL AID

As noted in the beginning of this chapter, admissions is the first hurdle; financial aid may be the second. Financial aid involves rather different considerations for older applicants and students than for younger students. However, financial aid is not always crucial. Aid is not as significant a factor at public institutions, where tuition is free or relatively low. Moreover, aid is not as relevant for members of religious orders, for their tuition and other expenses are usually taken care of by their order or by the university, if it is Catholic. Nevertheless, members of religious orders apply for fellowships or assistantships. Their order may be somewhat more willing to send them to a secular or even a Catholic university if their expenses can be provided for or reduced by aid from some other source. Some older students and applicants have accumulated some wealth and some women students are married to men with substantial incomes. Even in these cases, aid may have some relevance, but for other than financial reasons, as we shall see later.

Financial aid takes many dimensions. It may cover tuition only, or it may include stipends to cover living expenses. Lump sum awards may be used for tuition, living expenses, travel, etc. Aid may take different forms: fellowships, which often are granted on the basis of ability rather than need; traineeships, which are usually federally financed and may be quite generous, and may or may not be available on the basis of need; scholarships or tuition exemptions, which are often made on the basis of need; and loans, which almost always are available only on the basis of proven need.

While various forms of financial aid have increased rapidly in recent years in nearly all fields, there is still considerable variation among fields in terms of relative availability. In addition, some university, governmental, and foundation fellowship programs have stated age limits. For the great majority of fellowships, however, there is no reference to age in the literature describing their availability. Even when age is mentioned, the maximum is sometimes age forty or above. Moreover, funds are available through so many agencies and devices that even if some grants carry age limitations, older persons seeking aid may find many other programs available without such limitations.

The proportion of students receiving aid, as noted earlier, varies greatly among the different fields. The availability of funds is most generous in social work, where 95 percent or more of all graduate students have full tuition and stipend support, regardless of age or need. Indeed many institutions have found themselves with more funds than they can allocate. In the natural and physical sciences, the general level of financial support is high. In these fields, age limits are more common, particularly for doctorate programs, but do not seem relevant because of the small number of older applicants. The proportion of all students who receive various forms of financial assistance ranges from 60 to 80 percent in the social sciences and in some languages critical to national defense. The proportion receiving aid in the other humanities is somewhat lower, perhaps on the order of 25 or 30 percent. In a few professional fields, such as law, almost no aid is available.

Federal funds are now available to enable mature educators to obtain sabbatical leaves for training. This is becoming an increasingly important factor in elementary or secondary school teaching or administration. In addition, a number of programs offer fairly generous financial aid in support of a particular activity rather than a particular educational field. As a result, for instance, there are grants available from such federal agencies as the National Institute of Mental Health, stretching across many fields, including social work, teaching, anthropology, psychology, and sociology.

Some financial aid programs are of special relevance to older students. Columbia University's New Careers fellowship program has been mentioned. The Danforth Foundation and the American Association of University Women have offered fellowship programs for women to return to school. Mature federal employees have advanced training fellowships or sabbaticals available to them.

The function of granting aid to students is usually shared by departments, deans' offices, financial aid offices, and others. As with admissions, shared responsibility opens up the opportunity for private or special criteria to develop somewhere in the process. Thus the "blackball" phenomenon reappears; if a single individual in the process is adversely inclined or negative toward older students, they may be denied aid. On the other hand, in fields in which aid is plentiful, as in social work, any one person in the process would find it difficult to justify the denial of aid to an older student.

On the basis of our investigation, we found that age itself is usually not a negative factor when it comes to applying for continuing financial aid. Financial aid decisions are usually made separately from and after admission, although from the students' point of view entrance may be a function of obtaining both admission and aid. Many educators say that if they accept a student, they feel a responsibility to see that he does not fail to complete his education for lack of funds. As one put it, "We make no distinction between older and younger students as to financial aid. Each is assisted to the best of our ability, according to his need." Another said, "We just anticipate the school would finance doctoral candidates if they need it." On the other hand, some officials definitely and consistently favor the young students in granting aid, despite the fact that their school may have larger numbers of older students than formerly, and despite the fact that the availability of funds is recognized by the official as a factor in the increased attendance of older students.

Some institutions offer most of their aid on the basis of ability and performance. Since few of the older students are among the most outstanding, they may rarely be aided in these institutions. However, even these institutions will often find a way to provide aid to an older student who would be forced to withdraw without it.

There was some evidence that older students, particularly those newly entering graduate or professional school, are not aware of the now common practice for schools to bid for students by offering them aid. Young students, particularly better students, have learned that graduate schools will compete for them, and they often decide which school to attend partly on the basis of the amount of aid they are offered. On the other hand, as one dean put it, older students are satisfied just to be admitted or to get tuition exemption; the question of an additional stipend is beyond their imagination.

Older students tend to become aware of the availability of financial aid only after they enter school. Once they learn of this, they may pursue fellowships and traineeships as assiduously as the young. When they realize that fellowship awards have symbolic as well as monetary value, older students seek them as a mark of approval and a status symbol, if not for the money, and regardless of need. In other words, they acquire the values common among younger students.

Many fellowships are given to students only when they enter graduate study. Thus, the older person who is unaware of the availability and significance of fellowships until after he has entered school may find that aid is foreclosed to him. This is particularly true of many of the federal programs. However if a vacancy or resignation occurs in a fellowship or traineeship, an older student may be granted the balance of the award.

We heard fairly often that "older students tend to rely on their own resources. . . . They often plan ahead, saving for several years and arranging for leave from jobs and for a substitute income." One dean cited instances of older students who did not show up for several years after being admitted because they required time to get their financial affairs in order. Another said that older students sometimes say they do not feel "entitled" to aid, but there was some disagreement on this point. Another dean noted that older students tend to get their applications for aid in late, whereas young students tend to apply early and therefore tend to win the fellowships. In obtaining fellowships on the basis of merit, too, the lack of current or recent recommendations may be a factor working against older students until they prove themselves. If writings are reviewed, as they sometimes are, materials prepared some time ago may deal with older problems or cite arguments which since have been proven wrong or seem naive.

We were told of a few older students who did not request aid but asked for work to pay their way. This was not common, however. An older person usually has an income earning capacity greater than he could earn in the usual college job. If he needs to work, he often can get a job on his own at much higher pay. Older students may take junior part-time teaching or research assistant jobs, but more for the honor and experience than for the money. Age may even be an advantage in getting a teaching assistantship, especially if one has experience in a field related to the subject. However, it is not uncommon for older students to avoid a research assistantship if it prevents the rapid completion of their studies. For the older student, time is of the essence.

In many professional fields, older persons who are working in or about the field may be better informed than the young about the availability of aid. If these workers are interested in returning to school, they will seek aid, particularly through their employer. They even tend to accept aid as a matter of right, and would not consider going to school without it. For many employed persons, of course, aid is necessary if they are to go to school. The amount of aid available through employers is so great in certain fields, as in social work, that if an employee of an agency seeks admission without aid, the school may be suspicious of him. In fields in which there are many opportunities for aid, the school is often not involved in granting it. This is especially true of the government traineeships, which are awarded either through the public or non-profit agency employing the person or by direct application to Washington by the prospective student, as well as through the school. A significant number of foundation grants also are made on the basis of direct application. As a result, in some cases a school is not fully aware of the extent to which its students are aided.

A fairly common comment was that "nearly all our older applicants are prepared to support themselves for at least a year or two." Departments often will not aid an older student until he proves his ability, but then he is treated as any other student. It was reported to be fairly common for older students to run out of money after they have been in school for a year or two, particularly because they had not foreseen the length of doctoral study. This is one of the reasons that some deans are so careful to ascertain just what older applicants want to do and how realistic their plans are.

Because older students are less likely to apply for aid or because they apply later than most, they tend to rely somewhat more heavily on loan programs than younger students. The size of a grant or loan to an older student does not seem to present a significant issue. In general, the amount of aid is given on the basis of need. If one has many responsibilities, as do many older students, he needs and gets more aid. Indeed, one aid officer deliberately allocates grants covering both tuition and stipends to those with children (who are more likely to be older) and gives grants covering tuition only to younger applicants. An opposite view was sometimes encountered, that if a choice must be made between supporting a few students with dependents and many more students without dependents, the latter will be chosen.

Undoubtedly, the availability of aid is crucial to a significant number of older students. However, it seems fairly clear that criteria based on age are far less common in granting financial aid than in granting admissions. The most common response, as noted above, was that once the school has admitted an older student, it feels a responsibility to insure that he does not drop out for lack of funds. We found no direct correlation between the availability of funds and the proportion of older students in a program. Some programs, such as social work, have generous funds available and have many older persons. On the other hand, science fields have generous funds and have relatively few older persons. Contrarily, the humanities have relatively little funds available but have relatively high proportions of older students. Law and pharmacy, with relatively few scholarships available, have relatively few older students.

EXPERIENCE WITH OLDER STUDENTS

Despite the general tendency of university officials to resist older students, substantial and perhaps increasing numbers of older students are, in fact, attending professional and graduate schools. This raises the question of how well they have done in school. We asked university officials to provide us with evidence or opinions on academic performance of older students and other aspects of their school experiences.

We encountered only one piece of concrete data which provided the basis for generalizations about performance. The Association of American Medical Colleges has found that the proportion of students who drop out of its member schools for either academic or other reasons rises steadily with age. This is, of course, not representative, both because medical training is so long and because less than 2 percent of all medical school students are aged thirty-five or more.

Lacking concrete evidence, we must rely on the opinions of university officials. Although many of them refused to generalize, on the ground that one must always look to the individual or specific situation, the majority were willing to generalize. These opinions have validity in that they are the comments of officials in schools or departments which had significant numbers and proportions of older students. However, these generalizations can be projected to any increase in the number of older students only with caution, for the present group is exceptional.

Although the majority of officials generalized freely, their generalizations were often in conflict. For instance, some said that older students, particularly women, are less likely to complete a program, but others said that older persons complete their program more often than young students because they have much more at stake and cannot afford to fail. Others suggested that older students are somewhat slower in learning the subject matter.

The fact that older students sometimes have greater problems in adjusting to graduate school seems to reflect the fact that younger students usually are continuing a process of education, while older students were out of school for some years after their college graduation. Older students returning to the university sometimes have forgotten how to study. In any case, these adjustment problems were usually surmounted by the end of the first semester.

The officials often said that the earlier preparation of older students was not as adequate as that of younger students, particularly in mathematics. Some older students have less adequate research skills and do not use the library as intensively. On the other hand, we were told that older students have broader horizons and are more realistic and less naive. Their maturity leads them to use their time more effectively, we were told. Their contributions in the classroom are often valuable to younger students. Older students understand the problems implicit in case materials, while younger students tend to be somewhat less sensitive.

We were told that a few years of experience may be very valuable; longer periods may yield little added value. Experience is often not relevant in programs that stress newer theoretical materials, especially doctoral programs. On the other hand, some officials said that with a given I.Q., older students do better in newer materials than do younger students. Practical experience is more likely to be significant in social work, the other helping professions, and business schools. Even in these fields older students have much to unlearn, for they are burdened with preconceived but erroneous notions based on their own practical experience. Older students sometimes do less well in field work because they are inhibited, while younger students tend to dive into the learning experience. Experienced older persons sometimes resist accepting apprenticeship status in field work.

Some officials told us that the memories of older students were less facile and that older students tire easily. Health problems are more frequent. It was common to hear that older students are self-conscious, feel inadequate, are humble, and are afraid of failure, and therefore press harder. Anxiety presents a real problem, and some deans and faculty members try to counteract it by telling success stories involving other older students.

We heard that older students try harder and have more commitment and drive. They were characterized as being more determined, but not willing to take suggestions easily. We were cautioned, however, that young as well as older students may be rigid.

One dean pointed out that older students are not as fanatic about their field as some younger students.

It was frequently said that older students are conscientious but not interested in subject matter. They tend to be practical; they want to obtain their credentials; they are not interested in learning, *per se*.

The academic performance of some older students is affected by their other responsibilities in connection with their family, job, or civic and social activities. Emergencies develop more often. A person sent to school by his employer may be called back because of an unexpected development. We also heard of older students refusing to disengage from local political or social activities. On the other hand, we often heard that older students are, in fact, less distracted from their studies by social life. Dating and the search for a mate can be time-consuming for the young.

We frequently heard that it is rare to find a truly outstanding person among the older students. As one dean put it, "I do not mean that they lose ability with age, but as far as we can tell . . . they never had as much as our brighter, younger students have." There were exceptions, however. Occasionally we heard of an outstanding woman student who had returned at middle age, or of a business man who had returned for a Ph.D. who might well become a dean. Otherwise, it was rare to find among the older students a person on the verge of moving up rapidly to a position of prominence. Some might enter key positions in their former organizations, but these would be minor, not major leadership positions. This appraisal of older students as limited may reflect the fact that many were in fields that do not often get first quality young people, either.

A considerable number of older students who are supported by their employers or who are in school to earn credits for a higher salary, as in public school teaching, are bored or feel put upon by having to attend school. Such older students simply do the minimum required of them. School attendance costs them nothing in cash outlay or lost income, and they do not permit it to cost them much effort.

We also heard that members of religious orders are sometimes sent to a professional school even though they have no aptitude for further study. Nuns and priests tend to be conscientious at their studies, and if the spark of understanding is not there, they struggle through largely on the basis of effort. A few cases of real talent were uncovered among the religious, however. One notable example was a priest who found himself unsuited for parish work, and was sent to prepare for high-school science teaching. He turned out to be a first-rate chemistry student and his department was trying to get his order to permit him to seek the Ph.D.

We were frequently told that older students tend to present few problems other than academic difficulties. As one official put it, "They have worked most of their problems out." Another said that older students have learned how to handle their problems or, at least, to keep them to themselves. Older students were said to tend to be steadier, more reliable, and less "troublesome." Although some reported that older students often appear to be quite anxious, there was little evidence that this presented significant problems.

We were told that older students tend to be less vocal about their likes and dislikes. Young students in trouble tend to blame the program, not themselves, while older students were more tolerant both of the program and of themselves. Some older students used to exercising power tend to be self-assertive in school. For instance, they complain more often about disorganization in school operations. Older undergraduates, as in teacher training programs, sometimes protest about mandatory physical training requirements.

The question of the relationships between older students and faculty members aroused some interest. There were a few reports that older students sometimes seek special status or deference from their professors or try to relate as peers to the faculty. There were also a few reports of older students having difficulty in dealing with younger instructors, but this was exceptional.

As for relationships to other students, we heard reports of "clubby" behavior among older women students who feel a kinship with each other and have a common enthusiasm. One school official reported that older women with families are even more active than younger students in voluntary work, as in slum neighborhoods or in publishing student newspapers.

We were also told, however, that the key to successful graduate study often turns on how well one integrates with the rest of the students. It was frequently reported that older people gradually integrate, that they are accepted by other students, begin to lunch with them, talk over their common problems, and even participate in social activities with the younger students. As one dean put it, the more fully they accept their student status, the more likely they are to succeed.

We were told fairly frequently that older students do not seek advice if they have problems. There was some evidence that they may be more independent, make up their own minds, and go their own way. Indeed, there were even signs that they avoid the dean's office because they feel that they are in school on sufferance. On the other hand, it is not necessary to keep a constant check on administrative details with older students. They are more systematic and ensure that their affairs are in order. The older student, we were told, does not need a father or a mother figure, and therefore does not seek a dependency relationship with someone in the faculty or dean's office, as do some young people. We were also told that older students give a student body more stability.

One student personnel officer stated, however, that while older students present fewer nonacademic problems to the school, this does not mean that they have fewer needs. They simple have different needs, which student personnel services are not set up to deal with. The university administration provides no help with the kinds of problems they face, such as during orientation or in obtaining social contacts for their family. We were even told by a dean in a divinity school that older students often require more counseling than younger students, although the reasons were not clear.

Our interviews were striking in their lack of unanimity and the willingness to generalize without data. With some strong exceptions, the majority of university officials confessed that they had not seriously thought about the question of older vs. younger students prior to our request for an interview. In part, this reflected the fact that the officials were busy people, often with short tenure in their jobs. Over and over we were told that the interview was welcome because it stimulated thought on the topic. It must be reported, however, that a distinct minority was definitely uninterested, both before and during the interview. Understandably, these schools tend to have few older students. The majority had significant numbers of older students, and this subject aroused their interest. This chapter has indicated some of the lines along which future research of a more definitive nature can take place.

5. *Into School and Out*

TO DISTINGUISH THE EFFECTS of returning to school from why older students return, we must again turn to the students themselves. In this chapter we propose to seee how the process of reentry, school attendance, and ultimate departure from the educational institution affects the older student. We will consider the students' reactions to three stages: 1) withdrawal from previous responsibilities and entry into the educational institution; 2) educational and other experiences while in the institution, including the impact of school attendance on other aspects of the students' lives; and 3) the departure from school, the return to other responsibilities (usually work), and the student's retrospective evaluation of his education and plans for future study. In this way we hope to produce insight into motivation, as well as guidance on a number of policy issues with respect to professional and graduate education for competent middle-aged persons.

One of the striking aspects of this group of older persons is the short period of time they took to decide to return to school. As Table 5.1 indicates, fifty-eight of the seventy individuals in our group responded to a question on this point. Of those reporting, twenty-nine, or half, indicated that they seriously considered the return for one year or less. Indeed, ten reported that they had thought about returning to school for one month or less.

From these ten came such comments as: "When the idea occurred to me, I immediately acted upon it;" "It was a sudden decision—a matter of two days;" and "I remember that I made my decision rather suddenly." Two respondents made their decisions quickly because they were unexpectedly offered an opportunity

TABLE 5.1. *Length of Time Respondent Seriously Considered Returning to School*

1 month or less	10
More than 1 month, but no more than 6 months	11
7 to 12 months	8
More than 1 year, but less than 5 years	19
5 or more years	4
"Always" expected to return	6
No answer	12
Total	70

to return to school. One of these was applying at a college for part-time courses on a nonmatriculated basis, but was offered matriculated status by a dean during an interview. As she says, "The decision was made on the spot, in the dean's office." Another decided within three weeks after receiving a telephone call from a professor with whom she was acquainted who offered her a scholarship in his program. Some realized that their quick decisions were facilitated by long-range considerations. One said, "I don't know exactly, it was very quick actually. . . . I simply went." However, she went on to say that the idea that a return to school was possible had been in the back of her mind for some time. Another said, "I had been going to school off and on. The decision to go full time was short, though. The superintendent suggested my applying in October, I think, and I applied in November."

The length of time taken to reach such a decision can be more definitely calculated for those whose decision was stimulated by a particular event. In the case of respondents who reported serious consideration for "years" or for a long but vague period, we must question how serious in fact their consideration was. In many cases, however, the report of long and serious consideration was buttressed by other evidence.

Among the six who said that they had "always" expected to return to school was one woman who returned when her youngest daughter was six years old; she obtained her Ph.D. in three years. She reported, "Ever since I was a little girl I wanted to be a history teacher," and she had had her dissertation topic in mind for many years before she returned to school. The evidence is also fairly clear in the case of those whose return to school on a full-time basis was preceded by a long period of intermittent and part-time education. For instance, one who said he had always intended to return had entered a master's program three years after graduating from college and then studied eight years to get the degree. Eight years after that he returned for his Ph.D. A housewife-nurse earned a public health nursing certificate at age thirty-five after a year of full-time study and then continued to accumulate credits through intermittent and part-time enrollment. She returned to full-time study at age forty because she was well enough advanced by then to complete her bachelor's study in a year. Somewhat more unusual was the psychotherapist who, after completing a bachelor's in sociology and a master's in social work, went to work with the intention of returning for a doctorate ten years later, on the theory that he could thereby better combine theory with practice. Meanwhile, he continued part-time study in psychonalysis. Events delayed his return for his Ph.D. for fifteen rather than ten years.

Those who indicated that they had seriously considered returning for five or more years tended to be persons whose return in fact was occasioned by specific events. One, for instance, entered a program at the "first real opportunity," which came when her children were in school full time. She also faced a deadline, for one year later she would have been past the arbitrary age limit for entering the specific program in which she was interested. Again, an Army warrant officer said that he had considered a return to school for many years and in fact had gone to school part time for years. However, it was fortuitous that he was located where he could enter a special concentrated part-time program of study for a bachelor's degree just as he approached his retirement date. Again, an artist who set out to get a bachelor's degree at age thirty-six said that he had considered going to college ever since he finished high school. However, his hopes apparently took reasonably firm shape only after he found some success in lecturing and writing after age thirty-three. This seemed to trigger his return to school on a full-time basis.

The short period during which many respondents made their decisions was reemphasized when they were asked what preparations they had made for their return. Of the seventy cases, fifteen provided no answer to this question. Another twenty replied that they had done little of significance other than to apply and take the required tests. Thus, only half reported making significant preparations. Twelve of the seventy had to arrange or adjust diverse responsibilities, usually with respect to their children and sometimes with respect to their job. Another twelve persons prepared by some intellectual activity, such as taking courses, studying independently, and the like. Financial preparations were made by only nine persons and seven others made preparations so diverse as to fall into no classification. It is interesting to note that only five of the seventy persons sought guidance from another person about their return to school.

Even fairly straightforward and minimal preparations can be quite complicated, however. One academic official who received and accepted the offer of a sabbatical leave reported, "My wife and I planned for nine months. Making all the arrangements for the move, submitting applications for my school and the children's [school], renting our house and finding an apartment in [the new city, and] seeking employment for my wife were all time-consuming tasks." Another returnee had to ascertain that college credits earned some twenty years earlier were still valid and that her qualifications to teach in the public schools were also valid, for she needed an interim job. She also arranged for taking a test to obtain a substitute teacher's license, leaving her old job, and working for some time as a substitute teacher before she was prepared to return to her studies.

As noted earlier, those who had to arrange or adjust diverse responsibilities tended to be women whose problems involved care of home and children. Among men, the more common problem was to arrange either to change the nature of their employment or to obtain a leave of absence. For instance, two men arranged to become intermittent and part-time consultants with their employers. One exercised a maximum of careful planning and investment management to accumulate funds to retire the mortgage on his home, set aside funds for his children's future college expenses, and provide for family living expenses for the required two-year period of study. A dentist sold his practice. An acting director of a social work agency had to recruit a successor before she could leave to get a degree which would enable her to become a director herself. The return of one woman was conditioned on the institutionalization of a mentally defective son. The director of a nursery school had to find someone to fill her position as well as a maid to care for her home; and a schoolteacher's return to school was conditioned on obtaining a sabbatical leave, which depended in part on whether her employer could find someone to fill her position during the leave.

The respondents were asked to rank the general degree to which they had academic, financial, family, or other problems while they were in school, with the options ranging from "serious," "considerable," and "slight," to "not at all." Four persons in the sample did not respond to this question and thirty-one out of the remaining sixty-six respondents, or nearly half, said that they had no academic problems. Another nineteen admitted to slight academic problems. Thus, more than two-thirds of the respondents admitted to little or no academic difficulty while they were in school. None of the remainder admitted to serious academic difficulties, but sixteen, or nearly one-fourth, indicated that they had had "considerable" academic difficulty.

With respect to finances, twenty-one of the sixty-five reporting, or one-third, indicated that they had no difficulty at all. Another twenty-four reported a slight degree of financial trouble. Thus, two-thirds of these students reported little or no financial difficulty. However, twelve reported "considerable" and eight reported "serious" financial difficulty.

The question of family problems was not applicable to the fourteen who were not married. Of the fifty-two persons with families who reported, fourteen, or approximately one-fourth, reported no family problems at all. Slight family difficulties were reported by eighteen, another thirteen reported considerable family difficulties, and seven reported serious difficulties.

The respondents were also asked to indicate any other problems they had had. Only twenty-one responded, and five of them said they had no other difficulties while attending school. Several of the remaining sixteen complained of lack of time. A priest and a businessman indicated considerable difficulty because they continued in their previous positions while studying. A few mentioned difficulties with transportation and commuting in large metropolitan areas. An artist complained of a lack of "time for painting or reading for pleasure or just to spend time talking to my wife."

At a somewhat different level, one respondent reported difficulty because of illness, and another because her husband was ill. A few had difficulties which seemed at least in part psychological. As one put it, "It is only the unreal problems such as coming to terms with myself that caused trouble." Another reported considerable nervous tension, perhaps because he had considerable academic difficulty. Three had more vague complaints. One said that he sometimes had a feeling of futility, doubting that he would ever accomplish his ends. Another reported a "loss of morale" during the lengthy period of study. Another reported that, because she was forced to limit her social and community activities and had little in common with the other students because of the difference in ages, she suffered from a certain degree of alienation and isolation.

Three made complaints about their schools. One complained

about the rigidity of the formal requirements which prevented him from studying materials which would be more useful to him. Two social workers complained forcefully about their field training, specifying that it was geared to the needs of inexperienced students.

When asked whether the fact that they were older meant that their studies were easier in any way, fifty-two of the respondents, or three out of four, replied in the affirmative. Some thirty-four, or approximately half of all respondents, supplied reasons directly related to their age, experience, maturity, and the like. The balance stressed changes in their personal qualities which had occurred since they had last been in school.

On the other hand, forty-eight respondents indicated that in one way or another their studies were more difficult because they were older. For fourteen, these difficulties had to do with some aspect of subject matter. Ten complained of difficulties in memorizing and three reported deficiencies in research skills. Another eight were concerned with demands on their time other than simply the pressure of studies, eight reported difficulties with their study habits, and six reported difficulties in test situations. Four had difficulties involving stamina, health, and the like.

Individual responses to the twin questions of whether the fact that they were older meant that their studies were easier or more difficult provide more insight. For instance, one respondent indicated, "Ten years of experience in the field . . . certainly gave me advantages that a 25-year-old doesn't have. [On the other hand], studying at home with children has its distractions. I don't read as quickly as I once did and I don't find myself spending the late hours at study as I did ten years ago. Bedtime has to be 11 p.m. for me." Another respondent who said that his studies were not in any way easier suggested, "Age and experience might have helped at an institution less theoretically oriented. They did not help [here. My] difficulty has not been due to age, *per se*, but to the lack of continuity between graduate and undergraduate studies. The problem was most serious in the quantitative areas, such as statistics and mathematics, for many changes have taken place in recent years in undergraduate curricula. Also, one forgets a great deal of this material in fifteen years." A woman student said, "Experience rather than age, I believe, made my studies easier. Several years in the classroom, raising two children, and a backlog of professional reading, all helped. [On the other hand], I can no longer skim through a textbook swallowing all its ideas uncritically. I found myself arguing with the authors and questioning every theory. This took much more time than my usual acceptance."

Another respondent felt he had better perspective in some areas, but he also suffered from an inadequate mathematical background and "a reluctance to swallow my pride and admit ignorance to *some* younger faculty members." Still another said, "I think that being older and having already experienced 'life,' I am less restless than younger students, can concentrate better on my studies, and give more time to them. Younger students probably read and think fast and have more physical energy to cope with the more trying parts of the year, such as exam periods."

Another said, "I have better perspective and more confidence in my own judgment. Thus, I rebelled at the . . . hours to memorize [certain traditional materials] and time is proving that 90 percent of that . . . is irrelevant to my specialty." He went on to say that his studies had also been more difficult because "I felt utterly boxed up in class meetings. . . . These (except seminars) are anachronisms since Gutenberg invented printing. Yet social pressure made me attempt it since I wasn't sure that lectures were mere re-hashings of other's articles." Another said, "Memory is not as good as it once was and thus I have to spend much more time with my work. Also, I'm much more serious about the work."

Another felt that there was no way in which his studies were easier now that he was older. Rather, "they are more difficult because . . . mathematics is taught differently now in secondary schools and in undergraduate schools. I have had to acquire a back-

ground of this while at the same time proceeding with my studies."
Another said that he "could see problems in broader context" but
that he had great difficulty "with the simple problem of taking a
test. Tests presume ability to spit out things which rely on memory.
I never could finish on time [and] always spent too much time
making sure I was going in the right direction." Another felt that
he was more mature and better motivated to work instead of play,
but that his employment, especially since he was in a management
position, and problems with his family had interfered with his con-
centration. On the other hand, he said that while studies were easier
"the testing procedures were more difficult. Examinations in many
cases are designed for the younger students and aim too much toward specifics rather than the broader picture in the mind of the
older person who is trying to learn rather than to memorize for
examinations."

When they were asked to compare their performance with that
of younger students, the majority thought they had performed better than average. While only three thought their performance was
very superior, as Table 5.2 indicates, seventeen thought that they
had done considerably better than the average, and twenty thought
they were at least slightly better than the average. Only twenty
respondents ranked themselves as average, and just four reported
that their performance was below average.

The respondents displayed a wider range of feelings when com-
paring their current performance to their own past performance.
More than half felt that their current performance was at least
slightly better than when they were younger. Nearly one-sixth, or
eleven respondents, thought they were currently much better
students than formerly; another twelve thought they were not as
good as formerly. However, twenty-one or nearly one-third, reported no significant difference between their performance as
students when young and in middle age.

As noted earlier, roughly one-third of the respondents reported
no financial problems in connection with their return to school,

TABLE 5.2. *Comparison of Academic Performance of Older Students to Younger Students and to Own Past Performance*

Ranking	Younger students	Own past performance
Very much better	3	11
Considerably better	17	11
Better	20	14
No difference	20	21
Not as good	4	12
No answer	6	1
Total	70	70

another third reported only slight problems, and only twenty persons reported serious or considerable financial problems. One-third sought no aid whatsoever, but two-thirds did try to get one form or another of financial aid. About one-third of those who sought aid were rejected. On the other hand, some received aid without seeking it. As a result, five out of seven of the respondents received aid of one sort or another.

Most of these older students detected no bias for or against older students in the granting of aid. About one-third were unable to comment on whether financial aid was freely available to older as to younger students at their school. Of those who ventured an opinion, however, two out of three felt that aid was given as freely to older as to younger applicants.

When asked to evaluate the relative income and expense positions of older and younger students in general, nearly half the respondents were unable to comment. Of those who did, the vast majority indicated that older students tend to have both greater resources and greater expenses. However, they emphasized the greater expenses somewhat more than the greater resources of older students. Considerably more than half were reluctant or unable to compare *their own* income and expense positions with those of either other older or younger students.

The fact that half the respondents did not answer these questions underscores two basic points. Students tend to know relatively little about the financial needs and resources of their fellow students. Moreover, age may not be the significant variable here. Many younger students have a considerable support from their families and some have other sources of income. Moreover, the opinion of older students with regard to what they considered an adequate income in relationship to their expenses varied considerably. Some who were making $20,000 or more felt much pressed by their expenses, while others making $4,000 to $6,000 reported no financial problems.

The number of persons in an older student's immediate family and dependent on him is obviously relevant in any decisions he makes. The size of respondents' families prior to their entering school varied greatly. Fourteen respondents had no one living with or dependent on them. Among the rest, the most common family size was four. Eight students had families of seven or more persons.

The extent of actual dependency was reduced in some cases because others in the family were working or were only partially supported by the student or the student's wife or husband. Counting the single persons, those who were employed with no one directly dependent on them (an example would be a working wife), and those dependent on others, a total of thirty-six, or over half, were financially responsible for no one or for only themselves before they went to school.

Nevertheless, a substantial minority had considerable family obligations while in school. Twenty-four of the seventy respondents were financially responsible for four or more persons, including themselves, while in school, and eight were responsible for six or more persons.

Information was sought on the financial resources available to these individuals during the year just prior to their return to school and during their first year of study. However, twenty-seven respondents provided little or no information which would permit such a comparison. Of the remainder, three reported no change. The balance were divided equally: twenty reported a decline in resources and twenty reported increased resources, sixten by more than 10 percent. A total of eighteen respondents reported increases of $1,000 or more, and five reported increases of as much as $6,000. Among the twenty who reported a decrease in funds, all but two reported a decline of at least $1,000. Nine reported a decline of $2,500 or more, and one reported a decrease in income of more than $6,000.

The changes in financial resources were diverse. Twenty-four reported a reduction in their income from regular employment, but five reported an increase from that source. Nine respondents relied to some extent on loans, nineteen on savings, twenty-one on fellowships, six on assistantships, twelve on the employment of their spouse, and five on aid from their family. Eight received increased funds from other sources.

Because funds came from so many different sources, it was sometimes difficult to designate a central source of finances after these students returned to school. Of the seventy respondents, twenty-five relied primarily on their own employment and another six relied primarily on their own savings. Nineteen relied on their spouse's employment. The remaining twenty relied on other or mixed sources of income.

With respect to expenses just before and after entering school, thirty-two, or nearly half, were unable or unwilling to provide information about themselves. Of the remainder, ten reported a reduction in expenses and one reported no change. Twenty-seven reported an increase in their expenditures; for twenty, the increase amounted to 10 percent or more.

The most common areas in which expenditures were reduced were income taxes, clothing, and food expenditures. However, many reported no change in many types of expenditures. Of the thirty-eight who provided expenditure data, no change in expenses for rent or upkeep of home was reported by twenty-three, no change in expeditures for insurance was reported by twenty, no change in food expenses was reported by eighteen, no change for medical expenses was reported by fourteen, and no change in transportation expenses was reported by thirteen. Of course, nearly all respondents reported an increase in tuition and book expenditures. Of the thirty-eight persons providing data, increases of at least 10 percent for transportation were reported by fifteen, by fourteen for medical expenses, by eleven for clothing expenses, and by ten for rent and the upkeep of their homes. In dollar terms, the usual added expense for tuition was between $1,000 and $2,000. This was reported by thirteen of the thirty-six respondents reporting an exact sum, while eleven reported increased expenditures for tuition of $300 to $700 dollars. Six reported an increase in the cost of their residence of more than $1,000.

The attitude of a middle-aged person's spouse when he or she seeks to return to school full time or nearly full time may be a crucial factor. As indicated earlier, fourteen of the respondents had no spouse; of the remaining fifty-six, twenty-one had spouses who were highly favorable and twenty had spouses who were generally favorable. Attitudes were mixed in seven cases and there was an indifferent response in four cases. In only four cases did the spouse actively resist the return to school.

The students were also asked what effects their re-entrance to school had upon their spouses and children. This question was irrelevant to the fourteen single persons and only partially relevant to the five married students who had no children. Half or more of the remaining respondents denied that their return to school had any significant effect upon their children or spouses. No more than eight students indicated a negative effect either psychologically or in terms of the quality of family life.

In fact, a surprisingly large number saw their return to school as a positive factor, stimulating interest, raising ambitions, providing interesting family discussions, and otherwise helping others in the family. Fourteen of the respondents reported that their return to school had positive psychological effects on their children. Nine respondents concluded that their return to school had a significant positive effect on their relationships with their spouses. While some reported that the return to school restricted their "social lives," only fourteen reported a significant reduction. A few even said that going to school enhanced their social lives.

The generally favorable response of these students to their return to school in middle age is indicated by the remarkable finding that sixty-five of the seventy indicated that if they had it to do all over again they would follow the same path. Only two clearly regretted their return. Fully half of those who said they would do it all over again stressed the psychological effects on themselves or others in the family. Nearly as many gave reasons which were centered on their jobs and twenty-three indicated the pleasure derived from the intellectual aspects of their studies.

Thirty-nine of the seventy reported that they were definitely interested in further study, including post-doctoral study, and nine indicated that they might be interested. Of the forty-eight, twenty-three, or nearly half, indicated that their future studies would be related to special aspects of their future employment. Another eighteen indicated a desire to complete their degree (i.e., their current study would not produce a degree), or to get an additional degree in the same field. Relatively few gave such generalized responses as "to improve themselves" or "to gain advancement" in their fields. The most important single factor which would condition their continuing or returning to study in the future was the availability of support. A significant number, thirteen, indicated that their future return to study would hinge primarily on whether they would find the time.

Since all but thirteen of the respondents were still students, they could provide little evidence about what happens when a middle-aged student returns to work. The respondents were almost evenly divided between those who anticipated or had experienced problems in returning to work and those who had not. The most commonly experienced or anticipated problem revolved around adjustment to a new situation. However, twenty reported some concern with finding a suitable job. On the other hand, thirty-eight respondents indicated that returning to work posed little or no difficulty, and twenty-two of them pointed to manpower shortages in their field. Another twelve indicated that they were already committed to return to a particular employer. As noted earlier, eighteen, or approximately one-fourth of the respondents, were on leave from their employer.

The implication is that a decision to return to school is strongly affected by expectations about later employment. This may not be crucial for a married woman who will be supported by her husband if she has difficulty in obtaining employment. Many middle-aged men and women students who have been working and who must work are protected by the fact that they are on leave and are supported directly or indirectly by their employers. Most of the others are unconcerned about future employment because there are shortages or because employment is rapidly growing in the fields they are temporarily leaving or expect to enter. The most important problem they anticipate is not reemployment but, as we have stated, adjustment to a new situation, which is normal when entering a new and perhaps higher-level job.

Nevertheless, security with respect to reemployment may still be a crucial determinant of whether to reenter school in middle age. Relatively few persons are likely to undertake such a course unless they know or believe that they will obtain satisfactory reemployment. The almost endemic manpower shortages in the nonprofit and public sectors may be the primary reason that nearly all the respondents are either in or moving to it. The few exceptions among our group were self-employed or in fields where skills are highly developed and individual such as in advertising and consulting. It may be that we found few middle-aged students who plan to remain in or move into the profit-seeking sector because academic credentials are not critically important there. It may also be that those who might consider returning to school and then to enter or reenter business enterprises decide against it because of anticipated difficulty in obtaining satisfactory reemployment on reentry to corporate career streams. This may also explain why school attendance by middle-aged persons employed in the profit-seeking sector is almost exclusively on a part-time basis.

It is worth noting again that our respondents are those who have succeeded in returning to school. For this reason they provide little evidence of the barriers in the way of a further increase in full-time school attendance by middle-aged persons. They also provide little evidence or grounds for speculation about those whose applications for reentry to school were turned down and none about those who have made no efforts to return to school because they do not want to jeopardize their jobs, careers, retirement benefits, friendships, and positions in their communities.

Nevertheless, the general picture that these respondents present is one of considerable success as students, a minimum of difficulty in reentering school and employment, considerable satisfaction about their past, and optimism about their future.

One reason for their satisfaction and optimism has already been reported in chapter 3; half of the respondents are seeking to move in a generally upward direction; twenty returned to school in order to move upward within a professional field, and fifteen expect to enter a profession from a lower level occupation. The remaining half are making a shift at the professional or managerial level; eighteen are shifting among fields which are closely related or are accomplishing a major reorientation within a general field, and another seventeen are accomplishing a major shift in occupation or function. These new directions are also undoubtedly a source of satisfaction.

This chapter has traced out a series of findings which are consistently related to the satisfaction and optimism of the group. They are not a frustrated group of would-be students; in fact, a large proportion indicated that they returned to school after a relatively short period of consideration. About two-thirds of them reported little or no academic, financial, or family problems. Most thought their studies were easier because they were older, although some said that their studies were more difficult because they were older. Nevertheless, they tended to consider themselves better-than-average students. Practically all indicated that given the chance, they would "do it all over again," and the large majority either had experienced or anticipated little or no difficulty in returning to work. Since a high proportion were experiencing upward occupational mobility, and most of the remainder were moving laterally because of their intrinsic interest in the new field, their optimism and satisfaction seem warranted. Moreover, those stances are in some contrast to the mixed view which, as chapter 4 reported, university officials tend to have of middle-aged students in general.

6. Case Studies

A MAJOR CHARACTERISTIC of our group of persons who set out in middle age to make significant transformations in the level and types of their skills through entering a professional or graduate school for an extended period of full-time or nearly full-time study is its diversity. It is difficult to select a typical person, for middle-aged persons return to school for diverse motives and as a result of diverse circumstances. As chapter 3 indicated, by middle age differences in past education, occupation, family, and personal values and outlook are so great, permitting so many possible combinations and permutations, that we had to select nine separate classes of reasons for returning to school, most of which could have been further subdivided.

This diversity was evident in the analysis of the data given on the questionnaires returned by our group of seventy middle-aged students. In the answers to any one question, however, the individual characters and experiences of those who return to school at middle age were submerged. We therefore will present several case histories to make the preceding general and statistical analysis more concrete and individual.

To avoid any personal bias in selecting cases to illustrate the complexity of individual situations, a structured selection process was devised. First, all seventy cases were grouped according to the reasons that they returned to school: 1) because of intrinsic interest in the subject or field; 2) to acquire new or increasingly important skills in one's field; 3) to accomplish an earlier ambition; 4) to improve one's financial status; 5) to earn necessary credentials or skills in a field in which one is already involved;

6) because support, funds, fellowships, etc., were available; 7) because of one's own affluence or financial capacity; 8) because a change in occupation was desirable or necessary; and 9) other reasons. Then, all cases were listed in a spectrum of cases, with those most alike listed near each other. At that point, we selected every fourth case and came up with a total of seventeen dissimilar cases. We then prepared a case history for each of these, making no attempt to disguise the cases other than to avoid the use of the person's name or initials, his location, and any other fact not essential to the case.

Each of these seventeen respondents was asked to verify the accuracy of the written summary and to give permission for its use. Only one respondent refused permission and another did not respond to a request for permission. The remaining fifteen cases provide a reasonable cross-section of the study group.

INTRINSIC INTEREST

The first three cases were classified as those with an intrinsic interest in their subject matter and in studies, *per se*. Two of them were aroused by almost incidental contacts with undergraduate education in middle age. The ultimate ambitions of all three turned toward college and university teaching, and one is now a professor. Let us turn to the cases.

Case No. 1. Mrs. C.C.Y. came from a relatively comfortable family. Both her father and mother graduated from high school and her father became an official in a railroad trade association. Her younger brother became a telephone company manager. After graduating from high school at the age of fifteen, Mrs. Y. entered a woman's college. She missed one year because of illness, but nevertheless she acquired a teaching certificate in two years. She did not report when she married or whether she worked during the next fifteen years; in any case she bore a son at age twenty-nine and a daughter at thirty-three. After her daughter's birth, she became a schoolteacher. She obtained a divorce several years later.

She said that after teaching elementary school for many years, "My children were growing up and I felt free to 'do something.' I had no desire to remarry, and social life . . . bored me. I loved to study so I decided to take a 'course' [at age forty-nine]. Something clicked and I made up two years in one and taught at the same time. I had a 4.8 out of a 5 average, which made me happy. I love everything about the university—the people, the learning, etc." She completed her bachelor's degree in a year.

Continuing with summer and part-time study, she received a master's degree the next year and credit for several more advanced courses. During this year she was teaching full-time during two school semesters and maintained a nearly perfect grade average! She also worked in a research project and taught at a workshop. She has since been accepted in a doctoral program at another university.

She credits her success to her "drive," but she had made no specific preparations to return to school nor did she even give lengthy consideration to the decision. "I simply went," she said.

She had no academic or financial problems and received no financial help, but she paid little tuition since she attended a public university. There were no significant changes in her expenses when she returned to school other than increased transportation expenses. Indeed, since her salary scale was moving up, there was no financial pinch at all.

Her academic performance has always been superior, but she feels that her studies are easier now. She "goofed off earlier" but she now understands the need to organize her work and get it in on time and she is able to do so. During her studies, however, a major family success and a major family problem developed. Her son, who is a musician, won a major competition which provided further studies abroad. However, her daughter, who had been fifteen when Mrs. Y. returned to her studies, married a neighborhood boy when they both were seventeen and in the senior year in high school. The daughter later had a child, and the future of the young couple is uncertain. Mrs. Y. wonders if her preoccupation with school was a cause of her daughter's early marriage but concludes that she will never know. She would, however, do it all over again. As she says, "I love going to school, and I love to study and learn. I hope that it helps my career, but even if it didn't, I enjoy what I'm doing."

The second case describes a man whose interest in further education was more longstanding and more slowly aroused, whose actions have been both less spontaneous and more hazardous, and whose difficulties have been so great that he is one of the two respondents who have regretted the decision to undertake full-time study in middle age.

Case No. 2. J.B. was born and grew up in a small town where his father was a bank manager and officer. Both his parents graduated from high school, as did an older brother who became a skilled laborer. His younger sister graduated from college and his younger brother became a physician. After graduating from high school, he went to a neighboring state university for a year, which was followed by a term at a state college nearer home.

He quit college for financial reasons—it was the middle of the depression—and because he thought he wanted to get married. He took a job in a bank in a nearby city but did not marry until several years later. For about six years, he went to banking school at night on a part-time basis. When World War II broke out, he took a one-year evening course in radio communications and then joined the Merchant Marine as a communications officer. By this time his first child, a daughter, had been born and during the war a son was born.

After the war he had some difficulty settling down. He did not return to banking but entered accounting and office management for a series of automobile dealers, first in his home city and then in and around a different, larger city. Out of work in 1950, he took a purchasing job in a manufacturing concern at a salary considerably below that which he had earned before. After seven years with only slow improvements he became convinced that future prospects in this job were limited. He then became business manager for an automobile dealer at a sizable increase in salary. After six years, this employer entered another line of business, and J.B. obtained a job with another automobile dealer at a reduction in salary.

In his forties, he became intrigued with education. As he put it, "I was always dissatisfied that I did not continue my college education and get a degree. . . . In attempting to help my son in his high-school work I became aware of my own scholastic shortcomings and played with the idea of evening school for about a year prior to enrolling." His daughter had finished high school two years earlier and his son was midway through high school.

J.B. enrolled in a night school program in business administration at age forty-five. "My children were grown and I was making a comfortable income and had accumulated some savings [and] I decided to try adult evening college. . . . This reflected the exercise of an opportunity to overcome my considered 'deficiency' of education due to the combination of the lessening of responsibilities and an increase in financial ability."

Attending college aroused new interests. "In the exposure and and process of this learning program I became interested in the educative process itself." He was particularly stimulated by an instructor in economics. "My considerations came to 'toy' with the idea of graduate study toward a Ph.D. in economics toward the goal of college teaching. After receiving my B.S. with a straight A average I was convinced that I should gamble (considering my age) on a Ph.D. in economics, since I was confident that teaching at the college level would be the most satisfying vocation that I could visualize."

He applied for an assistantship at six widely scattered business schools. He thought that rejection or acceptance would serve as a valid check on his judgment. He was offered an assistantship at one university, a scholarship at a second, and a loan at a third. With the offer of the assistantship, which was from a public university in his home state, "the die was cast." His daughter was then married, his son was in college, and it would be relatively easy for him and his wife to move. He quit his job and accepted the assistantship. A year later he returned to the university at which he had received his bachelor's degree. It was a better school, and had offered him an assistantship with tuition remission and a somewhat larger stipend. The assistantship was renewed a second year with an even larger stipend.

When he entered graduate study the family income was reduced considerably, even though his wife took a part-time job and he obtained employment each summer during his studies. Some expenditures were reduced, particularly for household operation, food, and taxes, although the expenses of his son's college attendance, which were being financed in part out of savings, now required even larger withdrawals. However, from his point of view, his financial situation has been "permissive." He does not feel that he had financial or family problems, although he reports considerable academic problems and general tension.

Graduate studies have been somewhat difficult for him; he devoted many extra hours to mathematics, in which he did not believe he had a good foundation. He believes that he must put in many more hours of study than younger students for equivalent grade performance. He has also been somewhat unhappy with his program, for he says the courses suffer "from lack of integration . . . and have not contained cumulative benefit."

He is now well into the program and anticipates receiving his

Ph.D. within the next year or so. He reports that he would *not* do it over again if he had the choice. He has been under too much "pressure," for one his age. He is also somewhat disillusioned by the attitude of his professors towards classroom teaching. Moreover, he anticipates that he may have some difficulty in obtaining a satisfactory teaching assignment because of his age. "I am still somewhat naive and wish to 'teach' more than to 'publish.' This may or may not prove to be an obstacle. If it does I have confidence that I could return to automotive business management."

He is now more than fifty years old. If he gets his Ph.D. he doubts that he will be particularly interested in further graduate or professional training. "Possibly after securing a teaching assignment, [I might take] some courses purely for personal enlightenment and not 'grades.' "

It is interesting that these first two people, as well as the next one, spent their childhoods and earlier adult years in outlying areas; their interest in graduate education was aroused when they were living in major metropolitan centers. The first two came from small-town backgrounds but the next person's origin was more exotic. Only after he was in the metropolis could he express his interest in advanced education.

Case No. 3. N.N. is from a Middle Eastern country. His family was well educated; his father and two sisters became teachers after receiving bachelor's degrees, a brother took a master's degree and became a teacher, and a second brother took a bachelor's degree and became an engineer. His mother was privately educated. Mr. N. received a degree in law at age twenty-two. Thereafter, he practiced law for five years and then worked for two years in a governmental administrative post. Obtaining a United Nations fellowship, he spent a year at a British college, acquired a diploma, and married a European girl. He returned to his native country, where he was employed during the next four years by American agencies, first as an administrative assistant and later as a political analyst and translator. During this time, two sons were born and American support enabled him to spend six months in the United States to observe and study American life and institutions. Later, at age thirty-five, he and his wife and children immigrated to the United States. His law degree was relatively useless to him here and he worked for two years as a garment presser in a clothing store.

At the age of thirty-seven, he entered a full-time master's program in political science. "[I had had a] desire to pursue scholarly subjects . . . since boyhood. . . . Scholarly pursuits . . . were nonexistent in [my native country]. Coming to the United States afforded me a golden opportunity to pursue higher studies and develop my desire for scholarly work and attainment."

He had serious financial problems when he returned to school. The family's principal source of income was his wife's job as a nurse's aide, although his family sent him money and he later obtained a loan and fellowship from the university. He also had considerable academic difficulty, although he reports that by and large his performance was superior. After getting the master's degree in a year, he entered a Ph.D. program in history at the same university. He studied full time for two years and finished his dissertation in one more year.

Subsequently, he became an assistant professor in one small college and later associate professor in another. Recently, he was awarded a year's fellowship at an American institution in the Middle East to study and conduct research on contemporary intellectual trends there.

Despite the financial and academic difficulties he encountered, and the general problems created by the necessity for him and his family to adjust to a new country, he has no doubts about the wisdom of returning to the university. He says that he would do it all over again "because of my desire for learning."

NEW SKILLS

The next two cases were classified as those who returned to school to acquire new or increasingly important skills in their fields. Both are professors and both entered doctoral programs in mathematics. One is an economist, who offers well-considered positions with regard to his own return and the need that more professionals of all sorts return for advanced studies. The other had been a mathematics professor without the Ph.D. For both, intellectual and professional development has been a long, continuous process.

Case No. 4. K.A. was born on a Western farm to parents who never entered high school. One brother graduated from high school, a sister became a nurse, and a second brother became an accountant after attending college. K.A. graduated from high school at seventeen and, after a year, entered a state college program in forestry. His studies were interrupted by service during World War II, but he then completed his bachelor's degree.

After working two years for a lumbering firm, he entered an Eastern forestry school, hoping to obtain a more challenging position in the same field, preferably teaching. Upon earning his master's, he entered a leading department of economics to study for his Ph.D., planning to teach and do research in forestry economics. After completing the residence requirements, he became an instructor in forestry at still another university. Finding the teaching load too heavy after two years, he returned to full-time research. Three years later he completed the Ph.D.

In the meantime, he accepted a position as an assistant professor of economics in a college of forestry. After four years there, he accepted a position as an associate professor of economics at an urban Catholic university at an increase in salary. He had long ago "simply lost interest" in forestry economics and the new position provided an opportunity to work in different subjects. He first taught general economics, and a year later began to teach mathematical economics and econometrics. "My background in mathematics was weak so I had to correct this deficiency." He began sitting in on undergraduate courses in mathematics. Then he formally enrolled for a master's in mathematics at his university, and completed the course work in two years of part-time study.

He then decided to enter a Ph.D. program in mathematics. He had firm ideas about his educational needs and how to meet them. "My decision to do graduate work in mathematics on a formal basis (instead of just sitting in on courses) is based on [the fact that] I don't think that I could learn mathematics effectively unless I studied for credit, and had some short-range goals such as preparing for an examination." He also says, "Mathematical economics was developed primarily by mathematicians, and if I am to work in this field I have to become very proficient in mathematics."

He made inquiries about National Science Foundation fellowships but learned that they are ordinarily restricted to those under forty. He was then already forty-three. Therefore, he applied for a faculty fellowship at his university, and received a one-year leave of absence at half salary. He embarked on full-time study at a strong mathematics department nearby and he expects to finish his second Ph.D. relatively soon. He anticipates undertaking post-doctoral studies in his two fields at some time in the future.

This burst of activity began when K.A. was about age forty. In addition he married at forty-one and became a father for the first time when he was forty-three. He had to use some savings during his full-time study, and family expenditures for gifts, recreation, clothes, donations, trips, etc., were cut but not those for health, food, and church. He also had to delay buying a badly needed new car. The paid leave was absolutely essential for his return to full-time study.

He has been content with his decision despite some negative

aspects. The return to school was costly and it was viewed unfavorably by his superiors and colleagues. The time he spent in school could have been used for research and publications, and their lack may hold up his promotions.

On the other hand, he feels that his studies are essential for his future, for they will result in better teaching and research. "Professions are changing so rapidly these days that a few years after leaving school one finds himself behind the younger people. In studying mathematics I am merely anticipating the nature of conditions in economics in virtually all schools, five, ten, or fifteen years from now. I think that it is inevitable that people will spend more time in school. As our technology improves and makes more 'free' time available to us, I think that we are going to spend more time in school. I believe that it is wiser to devote our resources to educational pursuits than to leisure and amusements. Also, new knowledge is being discovered at a very rapid rate, and people must of necessity shift out of old and declining professions into the new and expanding ones. An increasing percent of the population will have college degrees, and also an increasing percent will obtain the Ph.D. degree. It seems natural that there would be a need for graduate work beyond the Ph.D. Post-doctoral studies are very common now, either for improving qualifications or for entering new fields."

The next case describes another person who returned because he needed new and increasing important skills in his field. He is different from the earlier cases in that he has spent nearly all of his life in major cities. He has experienced geographical as well as social mobility, for he came from a modest background. He is one of the few Negroes in our group of respondents.

Case No. 5. N.C. is an associate professor of mathematics. His father was a mechanic and his mother a domestic; the family has lived in a number of major cities in the South and North. All of his brothers and sisters completed at least high school and one brother is a physician. He graduated from high school at age eighteen and, after a period of military service, entered college and earned a degree in mathematics and business administration in three years. He then married and accepted a job as a postal clerk. Seven children were born during the next thirteen years.

At age thirty he started part-time study toward a master's degree in mathematics. A year later, he obtained a job as a mathematics instructor at a local college and began to study full-time. In two more years, he attained the degree, and then accepted a post as an assistant professor of mathematics in a college in another region. During three consecutive summers, he attended National Science Foundation institutes on mathematics at different universities.

At age thirty-six he obtained a one-year grant for full-time study in mathematics. When the year was up, he returned to college teaching for four more years. Then at age forty-one, for the first time, he entered a Ph.D. program at a leading department on a full-time basis.

He states, "My professional training has been . . . 'pieced together' over a long period of time. Perhaps this has been the main factor for my entering and re-entering . . . study. The changes in mathematics in the last several (ten to fifteen) years is another reason. The desire could not have been fulfilled had it not been for the various government programs." He reports few academic, financial, or family problems. Of course, his salary is not high, particularly since he has seven children to support. However, his Ph.D. study is being financed under a grant which maintains his full salary, and he has an additional grant from his state government. His family remained at home, and he used the extra money to cover his travel and living expenses in a distant city. He has enjoyed returning to school: he has been a successful student, he frankly enjoys the role of the student; and he is interested in mathematics. His present leave and grant will not be enough for him to complete the Ph.D. When he will be able to return to complete his studies depends on financial considerations but he does look forward to further graduate study.

INCREASED EARNINGS

The next case is one of the few who returned to school primarily to improve his financial position. However, he stresses the satisfactions he will gain from his added skills. The theme of slowly developing educational qualifications and career goals appears in this case, as it does in so many.

Case No. 6. K.T.U.'s father and mother were born in Europe and attended elementary school. His father owned a restaurant and his brother became an architectural designer after finishing college. K.T.U. pieced together the equivalent of two years of college at three campuses. This was enough to gain admission to a dental school, which he attended for four years earning a degree. After fourteen years of general practice in a suburban town, "I decided to enter graduate school to improve my financial position. During my many years in general dentistry I made a good living but . . . I thought I could make a better living with less work and anxiety. . . . Also I saw many children with malformed dentition and faces and . . . I thought I would be in a better position to help them as an orthodontist. As a specialist in dentistry, I believe one has greater status professionally among his colleagues and friends, etc. It took several years to realize [this]. Then too it takes several years of practice in dentistry sometimes to decide where one really wants to go in this field. Subsequently, I believe I will find greater spiritual and financial rewards in my new field."

His decision to return to school at age thirty-eight was influenced by an orthodontist who, while treating him, also taught him some basic orthodontic techniques. He inquired at two local universities but neither had vacancies for the coming year. He thought of waiting, but then applied at a third local university, where he was accepted. However, it was a year later before he reentered school since it took that time to sell his practice. In the meantime, he studied textbooks and after he was formally a student he encountered no significant academic problems.

He had a wife and one child, but his period of study created no family problems. Nor did he have financial problems. He had high expenses because he believes in "living more comfortably and enjoying life more," but he did somewhat reduce his standard of living. He relied on income from his investments, savings, the sale of his practice, and loans from a bank and the government. He is happy that he returned to school and feels he has gained a new perspective and sound goals in life. He expects no particular difficulties in reentering practice, although new working routines and applying new principles may make the first year difficult. However, there are many opportunities in orthodontics, including teaching and research. He might even go back for a Ph.D. in the future, but only if he decides to become a teacher in addition to maintaining his practice.

TO GAIN CREDENTIALS

The next two cases are drawn from among those who re-entered school in order to gain the credentials considered necessary for obtaining satisfactory jobs and advancement in the fields in which they were already involved. One is both a social worker and a psychoanalyst. He is unusual among the respondents to our questionnaire because he deliberately left school after reaching a middle stage in graduate study, planning to return for the doctorate at a later stage. Both he and the next case, a nurse, are notable by their attachment to their professions. Their interest in acquiring new skills was evidenced by their considerable part-time study when they were not engaged as full-time students.

Case No. 7. L.G.D.'s father and mother were born in Europe. His father attended college and became a manufacturer. His mother, who finished only grammar school, had been a minor labor union official. His two sisters attended graduate schools: one became an educational administrator and the other a senior biological research worker. L.G.D. acquired his bachelor's degree in sociology and then completed the classwork for a master's in social work. His plans for the future were quite complicated. He still had to write a master's thesis, but he immediately took a job. "I intended to work for about ten years, then obtain a doctorate. I felt that this would allow me to amalgamate theory with practice and most effectively use my ultimate graduate training."

As a result of practical and fortuitous circumstances, he was not able to keep his time schedule. When he completed the courses required for the master's degree, he married and entered group work for a private agency in another city, in part to be near a psychoanalytic training institute which he wanted to enter. Completing the master's degree was a prerequisite for this training. However, he was ambivalent about the thesis subject he had chosen and took five years to complete the task. During this period he worked part time as a Sunday School teacher and principal. By the time he entered psychoanalytic training, the length of the program had been increased from three to four years on a part-time basis.

Mid-way in this training period, he accepted a new job in another private agency which more nearly fitted his new skills. His first son was born while he was in training, just as his wife completed her own study for a master's degree in social work. Three more sons were born during the following nine years. His wife also took the same four-year part-time psychoanalytic training program.

After his training was completed, L.G.D. begain to work part time in clinics and to see a few private patients in addition to his regular job with the private agency. Two years later he accepted a job as an assistant director in a family service agency. In addition, he became chairman of a local professional association for two years. He was then late on his schedule to return for a doctorate and he was again delayed because his agency was hard-pressed due to the terminal illness of a fellow administrator and because of the arrival of his fourth child.

Even though he did not have the doctorate, he had for some time been receiving teaching offers from various universities, including some of the first rank. Some were willing to make time availabe for him to complete the Ph.D. He decided, how-ever, that he would realize more from the Ph.D. if he were a full-time student. He considered studying for a doctorate in social work, but felt that the financial returns would be too little for the time invested. Consequently, he entered a special Ph.D. program heavily oriented towards psychology and other traditional disciplines. He was then thirty-eight years old.

He reports considerable academic problems, not because of grades (they have been good), but because of strain created by his new role and expectations. There have been no overt family problems, certainly none with the children. Just before and after his return to school, the uncertainty had been somewhat difficult for his wife. He says he has had serious financial problems. However, the reduction in his own income was largely made up by loans, withdrawals from savings, fellowships, scholarships, and an increase in his wife's earnings as a part-time therapist. He worked part time during the first year because he received only a small traineeship, which may have been the result of his apply-ing somewhat later or because the school had some doubts about his promise. After a few months of study, faculty members encouraged him to apply for a much larger training grant, which he obtained.

He would return to school again, although he regrets the delay he permitted to develop. He looks forward eagerly to returning to work and anticipates no problems in doing so. Indeed, it is the other way around. For him, the problem has been to adjust to a student's lack of direct responsibility and control. He feels that a return to teaching, practice, and research will be a source of considerable challenge and satisfaction for him.

Case No. 8. Mrs. A.J.'s parents immigrated from Europe—her father when a young man and her mother when an infant—and neither had more than a grade-school education. One brother and a sister graduated from high school, and a second brother graduated from college and became a schoolteacher. A.J. has always lived in the suburbs of large cities. She graduated from a hospital school of nursing and married while she was in training. She worked until just before the birth of her son. Thereafter her educational and work experiences were brief and few until she reached the age of thirty-four. Her second and youngest child, a daughter, was then nine years old. She sought a job in a local health department which would lead into a public health nursing traineeship. Her application was held up for political patronage reasons, but was approved just as her prospective superior located an open traineeship for her at a nearby college. The traineeship provided for full-time college attendance for a year, and she took it rather than the job with a promise of train-ing. After obtaining a public health certificate, she worked several years as a public health nurse, continuing to attend college on a part-time and intermittent basis.

At age thirty-eight she returned to college full time because she was then within one year of getting her bachelor's degree in nursing education. She partially financed her studies by a loan to cover tuition for one semester. She states, "I've always planned and expected to have a career in nursing. . . . I have worked in public health and know that I am committed to this field not only because I accepted a traineeship but because I like the work."

Although she returned to school to complete her bachelor's

degree, which is the normal requirement for a public health staff nurse, she was so successful that her professors encouraged her to apply for another traineeship to continue graduate study. She got this support, and thereby raised her ambitions. Her ultimate hope is to get a master's degree in education and to teach public health nursing at the college level. She feels a strong personal commitment to contribute to her field where trained people are so badly needed. "Last but not least, I love the challenge involved in learning things. I get a lot of purely personal satisfaction from mastering something." Her grades have been good. She ranks her financial and family problems as slight. Her husband's income as a college professor was and is the family's chief source of support. As for her family, "I think they sometimes felt neglected or I felt guilty—I'm not sure which. They knew I was having fun. My studies caused lots of stimulating discussion around the dinner table." She anticipates no difficulty in finding a job after completing school, for "nurses are in great demand—any kind or anywhere."

FINANCIAL SUPPORT AVAILABLE

The next two cases describe persons whose return to study occurred primarily because of the availability of funds to cover tuition and some living expenses. Both had enjoyed considerable success in their chosen fields, and both felt that doctoral study was highly desirable, although for quite different reasons. Neither did anything about these desires, however, until financial support was forthcoming. The first case is one of the few in the sample who moved an entire family from one metropolitan area to another. His comments graphically illustrate the difficulties created by the move and show why most persons returning to school in middle age are limited to the metropolitan area in which they live and work.

Case No. 9. K.L.M. was born in a major city, but until he was twenty-six he lived in small towns. His father, a high-school graduate, had been a rural mail carrier. His mother attended college for three years and had been an elementary school teacher. After graduating from high school, K.L.M. obtained an associate degree at a small college and a bachelor's degree in secondary education at a small university two years later. While he was in the armed services, he attended a highly specialized school for six months. On his return to civilian life, he taught in a high school for two years, and then left to attend a large urban university where he received a master's degree in educational administration.

He stayed with this university as, successively, administrative assistant, director of adult education conferences, assistant dean, and associate dean. He also married, acquiring two stepchildren.

Ever since he had earned his master's degree, he had wanted to go on for the doctorate at a major university in another city, but this did not seem practical until he was granted a sabbatical. He reported, "I had progressed as far as I could in university educational administration without the Ph.D. Not being content to continue for twenty-five years as the associate dean, . . . my family and I uprooted ourselves from the comforts of middle-class [suburban] living . . . for the rigors" of the urban neighborhood surrounding the new university.

It was not an easy departure, for it meant leaving college, neighbors, and friends, dislocating the children, and forcing them to begin over in a new system. Fortunately, they were admitted as students in a special school connected with the university.

The departure involved considerable planning. He had to submit applications for admission to the university, arrange for the children's education, rent his house, find an apartment, and seek employment for his wife in the new location. He reports only slight financial problems. During his first year of study he continued to receive half his salary, but he then resigned his deanship in order to stay to complete the doctorate. His wife was employed as a secretary and they received a substantial sum of money from the rental of their home. He also held a minor research post during his first year. During the second year, he applied for a scholarship but was given a job as research associate, at first on half-time and later on a full-time basis. In point of fact, therefore, "we had more income to report than at any period in our lives." However, rent in the city was far higher than his former mortgage payments and the combined tuitions of husband and children were high. The family halved their clothing expenditures but little else could be cut. The only other offsetting factor was that payments on an outstanding loan had just been completed.

Although he reports considerable academic problems, K.L.M. rates his performance as superior to that of younger students in his department, and much better than his own performance when he was young. His major difficulties are distractions at home and an inability to read as quickly or to study as far into the night as he once had. There have been slight family problems due to their "rather severe living conditions," the limitations on the children's freedom, and his concern for their safety in the urban environment. His wife was very much in favor of his decision to return to school, and both have felt that the sacrifice involved is less painful than it would have been to watch opportunities for advancement pass him by. He anticipates no trouble in getting a job at a substantial increase in salary. He hopes to study again in the future in order to keep abreast of his field. This might involve a further period of full-time study on his next sabbatical.

Both this and the following case were people who satisfied long-standing ambitions to obtain further education when funds were available. The difference is that, in the previous case, the funds were a regular benefit provided by the individual's employer, while in the next case funds became available suddenly and fortuitously.

Case No. 10. B.B.C. was born and reared in Europe. His father, a high-school graduate, was an elected representative in the national government. His mother finished grade school. His three sisters and his brother all attended specialized institutions of higher education and became, respectively, a nurse, a regional political representative, a teacher, and a bank director. B.B.C. obtained a diploma in chemical engineering from a technical university. After a year of military service, he came to the United States at age twenty-six as an exchange student-trainee in applied research for a private company. Returning to his own country, he engaged in research for the defense establishment, but then resigned because he was unhappy with general working conditions and felt inadequate for the job.

Returning to the United States, he became a technical consultant for his former company, hoping to gain experience in research and development. He began to study part time for a master's degree in chemical engineering, and acquired it in four years. He continued to feel that he was not adequately trained for his work, and that his interests were too varied for industry. Although he was "looked upon as being the intelligent and well-informed expert," he had "a growing feeling of being a fraud," even though, he said, "My intellectual interests were greater and my views broader than those of most of my co-workers."

Then, at age thirty-seven, "a friend of mine offered me part of a National Science Foundation grant to do my doctoral study [involving] rather sophisticated use of computers, programming, and numerical analysis. I accepted without hesitation because it was a type of work I would have no opportunity to learn in industry, without change of job and without a substantial cut in salary. It would involve little economic sacrifice. . . . It offered an excellent opportunity for future teaching combined with work as an independent consultant, and it offered an opportunity for contact with the academic world and with people with strong intellectual ambitions."

He studied full time for a year, continuing with his employer as a part-time consultant. In two more years of part-time study, while working as a consultant, he finished the Ph.D. He then became a self-employed consultant in chemical engineering.

His wife, who also holds a Ph.D., contributed greatly to his decision to seek the doctorate by encouraging him, stimulating his intellectual curiosity, and reaffirming his values. He never had any doubt about reemployment, since he knew he could always return to his former employer and he had several other interesting standing offers. He reports no academic, financial, or family problems.

Besides his NSF grant, he received a loan, forgivable if he enters teaching. Even with these funds and his part-time consulting, the total resources of the family dropped in his first year of study, largely because his wife had to quit work for the birth of the first of two children born during his studies. Expenditures increased considerably because of tuition, medical expenses, and household help, and he drew heavily on savings. During the second year, however, he worked on a full-time basis and his wife was able to work, so that the family had considerably more income than before he entered school. Expenditures also increased, in part because they continued to have household help and the family moved to a more expensive home. Despite his relatively high income, he says that he would not have gone back to school without financial aid. He is happy that he returned to school and would do it again, but he has no plans for future study on an "organized level."

AFFLUENCE

How many would choose to return to school and leave a job and a successful career of many years? Not many, but the next case illustrates this relatively unusual group, which may become more common in the affluent future. This respondent had long wanted to return to graduate study, but his actual return seemed to be almost fortuitous. He is single and insists on maintaining his pattern of living, as did the preceding case, who was married and had children.

Case No. 11. D.E.K. had been in marketing research ever since he started to work after receiving a college degree in statistics and a year's graduate study in economics. His father had completed high school and was a salesman; his mother had attended high school and worked as a bookkeeper. His older sister did some graduate work and ultimately became a corporation vice-president. D.E.K.'s own college study had been interrupted by three years of military service. Starting work at a very low salary, in eighteen years he had climbed to executive vice-president, with managerial and professional responsibilities in marketing. During eight years of this time, he was a part-time lecturer in statistics at a graduate school of business administration.

When he was forty-two, it developed that "My business situation was such that I saw an advantage in seeking to change jobs. In reviewing my possible actions, it occurred to me that, rather than change jobs, I was in a position financially to support myself in school for a couple of years. Graduate study was something I had always promised myself in some vague future plans. At that time, I decided to make it a fact."

He considered studying operations research in a graduate business school, but settled on a Ph.D. program in mathematics because "I have always preferred to learn theory and develop application myself rather than to be taught application."

He had considerable difficulty in adjusting to the routine of study. In addition, because the basic approach to lower level mathematics had changed in the last twenty years, he found himself studying with people who had been prepared differently. "I have had to acquire [a new] background . . . while at the same time proceeding with my studies." He ranks himself as an average student and thinks that his performance is not as good as when he was younger.

He is single and reports no financial or family problems. His income was reduced substantially although he earns an occasional consultant's fee and has investment income. Some of his expenses were reduced but, with the tuition, his total expenses increased when he returned to school. "My expenses run high because I feel it important to maintain a certain level of living and maintain business contacts." He has drawn on savings and will continue to do so for two years of doctoral study.

He expects his future job to be at essentially the same level as his former position, but he will be able to take some new approaches in his work. In addition, he has begun to speculate about the possibility of entering university teaching on a full-time basis. He expects no difficulty in finding a job: "I have an established career and reputation and [a] growing professional career. My schooling activity will put me into an almost unique position in my field." He has been quite happy with his return to school. As for further study, he might take some course work in classical languages "solely for fun."

CHANGING FIELDS

This sample of case histories includes three of the fourteen who came to the conclusion that a change in their career fields was necessary or desirable. One, a former sales representative seeking a Ph.D. in anthropology, has had a particularly difficult time of it, both in his business career and as a student. However, he has persevered, seeking success through education.

Case No. 12. N.D. had been a sales representative. His parents were both born abroad, their education was limited, and his father was a tailor. His brother and sister, both much older than he, graduated from high school and became clerical workers. After high school, N.D. went to college and graduated after six years, including two years in the navy. He had intended to become an advertising copywriter, but he accepted a job as a social investigator because he needed a job urgently. A year later he accepted a better-paying clerical position with a specialty wholesaler, but only as "a temporary position as a means to earn some money." He also attended hair-dressing school, but withdrew after a month. A year and a half later he accepted a job with a manufacturer of the specialty product at slightly lower pay, because it offered an opportunity to become a salesman. His twelve years there were marked by slow advancement. His only other educational ventures were some brief guitar instructions and a course in the philosophy of religion, but he withdrew from the latter in mid-semester because he had difficulty in comprehending the material.

N.D. thought he was being groomed for a particular job, but his superior brought a relative into the company, obviously for the purpose of assuming some of the functions of the job. N.D. says, "I had lost much of my enthusiasm for the job along the way but I had stayed on because the future, in financial terms, seemed promising enough. But with this new chain of events, I began to reevaluate my situation. I suppose I felt I had to do something. . . . My original notion was to begin studying so that at age fifty-five or so, I might be prepared to take on some new assignment. . . . I was interested in psychology at this time. I vaguely thought about the possibility of training to be a marriage counselor. This meant the opportunity to do something useful."

He noted the satisfaction that he found through casual reading. He took some undergraduate courses in psychology and then entered a master's program in sociology part time, while working. He had no particular occupational goal in mind, but education, he said, "represented a source of hope. . . . My major problem was in rebuilding an intellectual foundation, one that had never been too sturdy to start with." He also took a brief adult education course in individual speech improvement.

He obtained the master's degree in three years but still did not feel qualified. "As a matter of fact, I was discouraged. [My wife and I] concluded that if I were accepted in a doctoral program I ought to give myself a fair chance for success by trying it on a full-time basis." He applied to a number of schools and was accepted by three. One even offered a fellowship, but he did not accept it because the school was thousands of miles away. One departmental chairman in a local university "suggested that I was a bad risk because I wasn't turning enough A grades," and rejected him. He was accepted by the anthropology department in the same university, however, and began full-time Ph.D. study at age thirty-eight with the hope of eventually writing about human behavior and teaching anthropology.

He had considerable difficulty in both the master's and Ph.D. programs, primarily because of his inadequate undergraduate preparation. "On the graduate level, I have had simultaneously to do both basic and advanced work in the social sciences." At first, he felt that younger students "were much brighter than I. It is only recently that I have begun to feel strength in these competitive terms." He says that his recent academic performance has been better than when he was young, primarily because his motivation to learn is much greater now.

He has completed his course work, and is preparing for comprehensive examinations. He says he is confident he will pass, but, pending their completion, he does not wish to comment about the future. However, in looking back, he feels he made the right choice in undertaking full-time study, even though it has "indeed been a difficult road." Several of his requests for fellowships were rejected, presumably because "my performance as a graduate student was mediocre [and because of] my advanced age.

A year after starting full-time study, he got a part-time job teaching undergraduate sociology and anthropology. "I was apprehensive before my first teaching experience, but I feel now that I'm going to be a good teacher in time." Social relationships were greatly reduced because he "affected a withdrawal into . . . books." Fortunately this was "not too much of a problem" because his wife, who encouraged him to go to school, has herself been a student in nursing education during most of his graduate study.

This last respondent left his former occupation because of a lack of success and satisfaction in it, and it seems fair to say that he has not yet achieved his goals in his new field, either. The next respondent, who is now in her third career, has had better results. She attended college after a first career, and returned to graduate school in middle age only after she decided that her second career was unsatisfactory. Her third career choice has apparently been satisfactory.

Case No. 13. Miss H.C. is a 45-year-old associate professor of history and political science in a small coeducational college. She came from a modest white-collar family in a small city, graduated from high school at eighteen, and went to work. By age twenty-five she had become a radio and copy director for a local advertising agency. At twenty-seven she entered college, earned a degree in history in three and a half years and then went on to get a master's degree in religious education at a theological seminary in another city, planning to enter the field of youth education.

However, each summer while in school she worked for her former employer, the advertising agency. When she received her master's at age thirty-two, she took a job for a church organization as associate editor of materials and magazines for college students. A little over a year later, she accepted a position as editor of publications and materials for the agency of her religious denomination which dealt specifically with higher education. After a time, she said, "I became dissatisfied with editorial work and the daily routine of office and editorial schedules and the lack of contact with people. Through experiences with campuses and student groups at both [my places of employment] and influences from friends associated with academic life, I felt a strong pull to either teaching or student activities."

Thus, at age thirty-five, she accepted a position as an assistant professor of Bible and director of student activities at a small college. "The dual role . . . gave me an opportunity to evaluate both the classroom relationships and teaching, and directing student activities." Within a year she decided in favor of teaching.

Realizing that she needed at least a master's degree in a subject and ultimately a Ph.D. degree to teach at the college level, at age thirty-six she entered a graduate school to get an M.A. in history, which had been her major in college. To support herself, she returned to part-time work as an editor with an agency of her religious denomination. Upon completing the master's degree, she accepted a position as an associate professor of history and political science, and immediately enrolled for a Ph.D. on a part-time and intermittent basis. She expects to complete her dissertation at about age forty-six.

Her expectations about what was demanded of her as a student and about her subsequent employment as a professor have been quite realistic. Indeed, she states that the decision to return for the master's degree was "a matter-of-fact decision." Part-time work made limited demands on her time and supplied reasonably adequate funds to meet her personal and academic expenses. While her education was stretched out over several more years than would have been necessary if she had not had to work, she does not regret it or feel she has been cheated. She has never found it difficult to study, although she was not a superior student. Even while she worked for the advertising agency she enjoyed studying and kept up with a variety of fields. She is perfectly happy in her profession now and expects to continue her studies in the future through institutes or independent reading in order to keep abreast of her field. Indeed, when she completes her dissertation, she hopes and expects to undertake special studies in England.

In the third case in which a change of career seemed necessary, our respondent did not seem to be as dissatisfied with her basic career choice as she was with the particular type of work for which she was best fitted. Thus her return to school was primarily to gain the skills to enable her to effectively shift from teaching suburban tots to urban, deprived, pre-school children.

Case No. 14. T.C.F. has always been interested in working with children. Her father graduated from the eighth grade and became a business executive. Her foreign-born mother completed high school, her younger brother completed college, her husband did some graduate work and is a federal employee, and her oldest son is a college music major. Three years after high-school graduation, she completed a bachelor's degree in psychology and then married. She continued to study toward a master's for a year but left at the urging of her faculty adviser to become a director of a wartime nursery school because of the great shortage of nursery teachers. When her husband returned after the war, she left her job and bore two sons in four years. When the youngest was thirteen years old, she accepted a job as a nursery school teacher, and two years later accepted an offer as a nursery school director.

However, she became concerned that her age (then forty-one) was a limiting factor in working with pre-school children and that her "years of active participation in the classroom are numbered." She said, "I wanted to prepare myself for some other aspect of early childhood education. I am still not certain what that will be—directorship, teaching future teachers, supervision, research—or what. Another factor in my decision to return to school was my desire to work with the 'disadvantaged' child and the realization that I needed further knowledge to do so. Years of middle-class suburban living and teaching left me ill-equipped to teach the deprived, urban child. The last factor was the advice of a professional in my field. She suggested that I return to school before I became too entrenched as a director of a suburban school."

After six months of serious consideration she applied to her former university department for permission to resume study for a master's but learned that they now offer only the doctorate. She then turned to another local university and was accepted in a master's program in early childhood education. They also gave her an assistantship with full tuition and stipend, in return for miscellaneous services. She had no academic or financial problems and only slight family problems. Her academic performance was superior to that of her younger classmates and also better than her own performance at a younger age, primarily because she was "more dedicated."

Her own income dropped when she became a graduate assistant, but this was partially offset by an increase in her husband's salary. Expenses climbed, in part because of the son's college tuition and his music lessons, and it was necessary to utilize their savings. Social life has been curtailed, but her husband has been very encouraging and extremely cooperative. The whole family has been proud of her and she "never heard one complaint when I had to retire to my desk to study."

Returning to work as a Head Start teacher has required an adjustment, for "after a year in a vital university intimately involved in urban problems, I find myself isolated in a classroom with practically no opportunity to exchange ideas with others similarly employed." She definitely enjoyed her graduate study and she felt it was a challenge and enlarged her horizons. She now wants to become a Head Start director and later a college teacher in child development. She is also considering further study because there is so much to learn and she hopes to be able to contribute to her field. If her hopes to become a university instructor begin to take shape, she will undertake further study.

A MULTITUDE OF REASONS

One of the cases which we found difficult to classify by the schema of chapter 3 is presented below. It was the only case of the seventy in which returning to school was a direct outgrowth of difficulties and dissatisfaction within the family.

Case No. 15. Mrs. L.S.F.'s father had a degree in chemical engineering and was director of a technical research foundation. Her mother had completed high school. Her brother and sister completed college; her brother became owner and editor of a publishing firm and her sister is a secretary. After high school, Mrs. F. went to college, transferred to another college for her sophomore year, and returned to her first college to get a degree in sociology. After one more year in a leading secretarial school, she worked for less than a year as a secretary to the director of advertising of a national firm. She left this firm to enter the WAVES for reasons of patriotism, money, and adventure and served as a full lieutenant in a staff position.

She had married, and after the war she and her husband moved to a university city where he became a student. For three semesters, she studied interior decorating but then she became a secretary in the university because the money was needed and she did not have enough to do in the apartment. During this time she also attended law school at night for three years.

After several jobs in the university complex over the next several years, she finally left for the birth of her first son. A second son, born two years later, was retarded and hyper-active. Meanwhile, her husband completed his studies and they moved to other cities as he pursued his career. However, he became "unsettled in his work and unrealistic in financial matters." They were going heavily into debt.

When the youngest child was four years old, she decided that it would be necessary to institutionalize him and for her to return to school "to prepare myself for financial independence and to help substitute (through being a teacher) for the family I never was going to be able to have." Caring for a hyperactive child and the lack of a satisfactory relationship with her husband weighed heavily on her. She had been elected to Phi Beta Kappa while in college and, she knew, "I could achieve satisfaction from returning to school and making my future more secure both financially and 'coming alive' again."

Before deciding on teacher training, she considered graduate study in social work or further work in sociology. She even took a temporary part-time secretarial job in a medical social work setting to examine that field more closely, but it depressed her. Moreover, public school teaching provided a time schedule which would permit her to fulfill the needs of her first son.

She institutionalized her second son, obtained a tuition scholarship, and at age forty-two became a full-time student. In one year, she got her master's degree in education. Because of the heavy institutional expenses for the retarded son and also to prepare for her older son's college expenses, she became a public school teacher. However, she became disappointed with the faculty and administrative personnel because of "their bigotry, resistance to innovation, and lack of professional attitude." After teaching for a year and a half, she obtained a graduate assistantship at her university which provided tuition and a stipend in exchange for part-time work and permitted part-time study for a doctorate in educational psychology. After making a good scholastic average in the first year, she got a scholarship and fellowship which permitted full time study. She has had no academic problems. She would have had serious financial problems except for the aid she has received. She rates her family problems as serious, both because of her son and continuing difficulties with her husband. He has been quite agreeable and even encouraging concerning her studies, but there has been continuing conflict with respect to care of the home and the two boys. However, she believes that her return has had a psychologically excellent effect upon her husband and son in "forcing [them] to become more self-reliant and forcing me to make them assume their own responsibilities. It is the best thing that could have happened to me psychologically (bringing worthwhile purpose and continuing growth into my life again), maritally (breaking an unhealthy mutual dependency pattern), as a mother (forcing my son to face some realities and take responsibility), and, I hope, financially."

For these reasons, she would do it all over again. However, she has not been happy with her program of study, because "too little time [has been] given to absorbing and discussing what we are rushing through and too much red tape and preoccupation with technicalities of degree and department requirements. Everyone, faculty and students, is trying too hard and the joy is gone from teaching and studying."

Despite the difficulties which hampered a few, these case histories project an atmosphere of satisfaction and success. Most of these middle-aged students have had a reasonable time in their new roles and feel happy and confident about the future. Of course, this sample may be biased because those with great difficulties are unlikely to respond to a questionnaire such as ours, and those who do respond tend to minimize their difficulties. This does not alter the fact that professional and graduate study has been a source of satisfaction and reward for a significant number of persons entering or reentering these programs in middle age. This is the unifying theme which runs through the majority of what are an otherwise diverse set of case histories.

7. Implications for Manpower
and Educational Policy

THE BASIC PREMISE of this study has been that the need for substantial changes in the nature of the careers of persons at a professional level is appearing and will probably be more important in the future. The underlying causes of this need seem to be the rapid growth in the number of persons in the professions, the increasing extent to which professional skills are acquired in educational institutions, rapid changes in the content of the professional fields, the emergence of many new specialties within fields, and flux in the number of professional level positions in different fields, industries, and enterprises. In light of these trends it appeared that there might be problems in finding an opportunity to change one's career by attending a professional or graduate school in middle age. Given the financial and other pressures of middle age, moreover, it might still be unrealistic for middle-aged people to attend professional or graduate school, even if they could gain admission.

This study has been directed at a limited number of questions implied by the above formulation. However, the results of the study tend to allay the fear that severe problems were emerging; in fact, they turn our attention to many more optimistic possibilities.

In particular, it appears that universities are much more flexible than one might have thought. Although there has been and continues to be significant resistance to middle-aged applicants, the fact is that a relatively large number of middle-aged men and women are now in these schools. The evidence is also fairly strong that universities, employers, and professional associations in general have shown an active concern and response to the need for part-time education as a means to upgrade skills slowly or to acquire needed information and skills as new techniques and knowledge emerge which are relevant to the different professions and management. These part-time and incidental educational opportunities are offered by universities, employers, or professional associations, housed in the facilities of any of the three, and financed by any of the three. While there are undoubtedly problems engendered by such part-time programs, in general there seems to be no substantial difficulties in the way of taking advantage of opportunities to make adjustments in the nature of one's professional skills.

Rather than uncovering problems, the present study has uncovered many interesting and optimistic possibilities. These primarily have to do with the continued development of people through middle age. This in itself creates new issues which should be of concern to guidance specialists, psychologists, leaders of the professions, employers, educators and educational planners, and those concerned with manpower in general.

From the point of view of those concerned with guidance, the fact that significant numbers of older persons are entering or reentering professional or graduate schools enlarges the concept of occupational choice. It reemphasizes earlier findings that the choice of an occupation is not a single decision. Rather, the cases here demonstrate that occupational choice is a process which for many people continues until much later than was previously thought. At one time, occupational choices appeared to be firmly made quite early in life. Only the few who were unsettled or who found they had made unwise choices would shift as late as thirty years of age. By the late thirties, it has generally been assumed, everyone is more or less settled in a life role.

Instead we find that the process of occupational choice many actually go on until much later, even into the fifties for some and for a few until after they are sixty years old or more. This is true, although there are increasingly important practical reasons against changing one's career as one grows older, particularly if it involves a considerable investment of time, money, and effort. In particular, as one grows older the amount of energy that an individual has tends to decline, as does the work life during which one can expect to recoup his investment. Nevertheless, significant numbers of middle-aged people are making new choices to invest in themselves. The older one grows, the more each person and his choices tend to be distinctive. By the time he enters middle age, each person has had a highly individualized series of educational, employment, social, and psychological development experiences. Each person tends to become more and more differentiated from others with regard to the nature of the family relationships and responsibilities to which he is subject and to which he responds.

For women particularly, the occupational choice process is now elongated. Indeed, for many women, occupational choice must be highly tentative while they are young, for the exigencies of courtship, marriage, and family life will greatly affect their work life, often in unexpected ways. Uncertainty inhibits investment in the accumulation of skills. This is in addition to the profound barriers to development which result from the reciprocal, negative attitudes of girls and their potential husbands toward carrers for women, as well as various social pressures from parents, school, family, employers, etc. For many women, however, the question of an occupation and employment almost automatically reopens in middle age. The reopened choice situation may contain fewer uncertainties for many women, when compared to their youth, because their personal responsibilities are reduced and their futures are somewhat more predictable.

The intriguing aspect of this study is that similar factors are affecting an increasing number of men. Some in military service and certain kinds of governmental employment retire as a matter of course during their late thirties or forties. Others find, because of economic, technological, or other changes affecting their employment, that it is convenient, attractive or necessary to leave their place of work and possibly their occupation. Thus, many, perhaps an increasing number of, men find that the choice of an occupational role is reopened. They also find a second choice not too difficult, particularly if they have access to, or can provide, the financial support necessary to acquire the skills which are essential to changing their occupation.

However it is an exaggeration to suggest that every person must be prepared for two or more careers. Some commentators have even urged that each person be prepared for six careers, but this is clearly not realistic. The processes of change which affect an individual during his lifetime, whether they have to do with his employer, his occupation, or his relationships with his employers, are usually handled with a minimum of difficulty, particularly for professional personnel. Most such changes are within a field of work and can hardly be called a change in career. Even when one changes his field, it is often unnecessary to seek additional training. On the other hand, the evidence is quite clear from the present study that many and perhaps an increasing number of persons are making major decisions with respect to their style of life and with regard to whether they would benefit from substantial education and retraining in order to enter a new field.

The present study also has interesting implications for developmental psychology. The fact that a certain number of professional people—the exact proportions are still unclear—continue to grow and change in their capacities, understandings, interests, and values is a point which has been little noted in the literature. Psychologists have been prone to deal with averages and the typical case. Those who return to full-time education in middle age are certainly not typical; one might question whether they ever will be typical. However, this small group and others like them who grow and change throughout the major part of their lives deserve separate examination on their own terms. It may be, as H. C. Lehman concludes, that the most creative years are usually between the ages of thirty and thirty-nine.[1] On the other hand, Bloom and others emphasize the importance of the general environment in the continued development of verbal skill and general intelligence in middle age.[2] Those who enter or reenter professional schools in middle age may be the products of special environments. On the other hand, the universities themselves represent environments calculated to produce change.

From the point of view of guidance, it is interesting to observe the relatively short time that most of these middle-aged students spent in preparing for their return to school. The majority did relatively little planning. For many, the return to full-time school came either because of a sudden change in their circumstances or because they became caught up in the process of education after taking courses on a more or less incidental basis. We have heard about young people who make supposedly crucial decisions with respect to their education and careers on relatively short notice and without deep thought. These supposedly shortsighted decisions have been "explained" by the fact that they were made by inexperienced, uninformed youths under a variety of adolescent social and psycho-sexual pressures. The evidence of this study suggests, however, that difficulties in making long-run plans may be more fundamental and are certainly not restricted to adolescents. In a dynamic society and economy, with a constantly unfolding opportunity structure, within which individuals themselves are constantly developing their interests, capacities, and

[1] H. C. Lehman, *Age and Achievement* (Princeton, Princeton University Press, 1953).
[2] Benjamin S. Bloom, *Stability and Change in Human Characteristics* (New York, Wiley, 1964), p. 81.

personal situations, firm long-range plans may often be unrealistic.

Of course, our study has direct implications for the guidance of the young. They need to be made aware of the long lifetime which stretches ahead of them. Although some in our study who returned to school in middle age might have found that step unnecessary if they had received better guidance and made better educational and occupational choices while they were young, the number in that situation was not significant. Rather, the study emphasized the unpredictability of the future. Young people should be advised that the choices they make while young are not irrevocable. In fact, a choice to undertake more or different education to change the contour of one's career can be made at almost any time in one's life. The feasibility of these choices depends on the strength of the desire and the circumstances in which one finds himself. It is also clear that young people need to know more about the possibilities of continuing growth and challenge throughout their lives.

Our group of middle-aged professional and graduate students provide new models for both the young and the old. This will undoubtedly have its greatest effect at some time in the future, when the present group of young university students themselves approach middle age. Their return to the university may be further encouraged by continuing increases in affluence, leisure time, ease of commutation, and the ubiquity of higher educational facilities.

To manpower specialists and leaders of the professions, middle-aged persons may represent a significantly larger potential pool of new manpower for fields in short supply than they were previously considered. Returning teachers have played a major role in meeting the manpower needs of the educational system over the last two decades. Moreover, professional leaders in social work have been particularly concerned with promoting social work as a second career. Such efforts need to be expanded and broadened, since many who were never able to enter a profession when they were young may now find this option open to them. In the light of increasing needs for teaching personnel in junior colleges, colleges, and universities in the future, it would be well to attract middle-aged persons with bachelor's or master's degrees to undertake an additional period of study in order to qualify for teaching at this level. In particular, those in technical fields may find it attractive to return to teaching in the basic and applied sciences.

It is not clear how many people would, if the conditions were right, embark upon a period of full-time professional or graduate study in the middle age. Those who are being accepted at universities today may be the more highly qualified among potential middle-aged students. If so, expanding the number of middle-aged students would merely dilute the quality. However, the evidence of this study suggests that so many erratic factors now determine who applies, who is admitted, and who finally enters school that there may be many more able persons who could profitably enter. If so, the number of older students could expand considerably before the basic contours, in terms of quality and expected results, would change markedly for the worse.

It may be that employers of middle-aged persons who have completed professional or graduate study do not give their placement sufficient attention. Both older and younger persons with new credentials need to be placed where they can continue their development. Of course, a young person is not exactly the same as an older person. The conditioning process to which inductees in a profession are ordinarily subjected ought to be sensitive to individual differences; middle-aged persons are likely to exhibit a broader range of differences in skills, in judgment, and in other attributes. Arbitrary practices with respect to the hiring and advancement of professionals based essentially upon age have no place in any properly organized career system.

The implications for education and educators are manifold.

The fact that one can return for advanced education in middle age places a premium on the quality of early education. We frequently heard complaints that the early education of older entrants to professional and graduate schools was deficient. The implication was that a return to advanced studies in middle age would be easier if greater emphasis had been given to fundamentals and to theoretical approaches in undergraduate and earlier education. This does not settle the issue, however. The deficiencies of many of the older students were primarily a function of the simple passage of time; the concepts and styles of analysis and thought in various academic subjects had developed and changed while they were out of school. A more fundamental or theoretical education when they were young would not have overcome these types of changes.

Increased emphasis on fundamental or theoretical education as preparation for a lifetime may be of little value to some people. Fundamental or theoretical education is not particularly meaningful to those who find their ways to understanding only by going from the particular to the general. For such persons, occupational education stressing practical approaches is a better way to develop understanding of and stimulate an interest in more generalized and theoretical materials. As a practical matter, moreover, the opportunities to acquire a general background at the college level are good in most metropolitan areas. This means that if a middle-aged person needs to acquire new skills and concepts in order to return to professional or graduate school, it can usually be accomplished relatively easily.

With regard to university admissions policies, this study has raised fundamental questions about the appraisal of older applicants and students. The general lack of evidence about the qualities which persons of different ages bring to or take out of the educational process and their performance in school is a serious matter. However, this deficiency is part of the general weakness of our conventional appraisal instruments for dealing with persons whose backgrounds differ in any significant respect from the average.

This is quite aside from any jaundiced view of the admissions process in general. In particular, there is room for concern with the relative looseness of the process; the lack of clear criteria with respect to students of any sort; the great number of individuals involved in admitting students, each with his own set of private criteria; and the rather clear evidence that, to some degree, favoritism and inside connections play a part. We do not seem to have realized that admission to graduate or professional school is no longer a private decision. Rather, it is involved with the public interest and the long-run welfare of the country and of individuals, and it is, moreover, heavily supported with public funds. In these circumstances, evidences of favoritism, discrimination on whatever grounds, and sheer obscurantism in the admissions process can only arouse searching questions.

Indeed, one may question whether any process of exclusion prior to entrance ought to play a heavy role in determining who is to go through the educational machinery. Education is a tryout experience for each individual. Middle-aged as well as young persons nearly always have some uncertainty as to their capacity and the direction in which they wish to move. They use school as a means to try themselves out. The ultimate test of the ability to do the educational task is the doing of it.

In effect, this argues for a more open enrollment policy than now prevails, with a correspondingly increased emphasis on screening out students who are not performing satisfactorily. This runs counter to current thought, which argues that it is a waste to admit people who subsequently drop out and that the best system is one which admits only those who ultimately graduate. A high completion rate may reflect a highly accurate selection process. However, it may reflect a highly inefficient screening-out process because of standards so strict that they deny entry to many potential graduates. This issue deserves more investigation.

One can overstress the desirability of middle-aged persons returning to school on a full-time basis. Some people seek to find in education a way to overcome their lack of success in other aspects of their lives. There are always a certain number of people who are unable for psychological or other reasons to make a proper evaluation of themselves and their future careers and who, therefore, turn out to be bad risks for an educational institution. Until the problem has been researched in depth, however, there is little reason to believe that these people are found relatively more frequently among middle-aged applicants than among the young. Indeed, older applicants may make more accurate self-appraisals than the young.

The fact that significant numbers of older people are going to school, and that even more might if opportunities were available, argues for increased emphasis on the expansion of educational facilities in urban metropolitan areas. In many parts of the country, the major educational institutions are located in rural areas, while the great majority of the population live in urban areas. If educational opportunities are to be available to more middle-aged persons, the facilities must be near their homes. This is true whether they will attend on a full-time or part-time basis.

The present study, although primarily of full-time students, emphasizes the importance of part-time educational opportunities. Part-time educational opportunities are particularly significant in those fields where the developmental process requires that one remain in a particular track. Part-time educational opportunities are also significant wherever career systems are such that it is difficult to leave employment and return while maintaining one's privileges and position in the promotion system.

Part-time education also plays a crucial role by providing an opportunity for those who might want to return to professional or graduate school but who are not sure of their capacities or interest to test themselves. Moreover, many people become interested in a full-time program only after being aroused by part-time study.

This emphasizes how important it is to keep open the opportunity to transfer from part-time to full-time programs. In many colleges and universities, the adult or extension division is so separate from the regular full-time program that it is difficult for older students to shift to a full-time schedule if they wish to complete their program of studies more rapidly.

Our study has also raised the question of what might be called "feasible" units of education. The length of time required to gain credentials is understandably a major factor affecting educational and occupation choices. Older people hesitate to undertake a long program of study. There are two principal reasons for this. One is the length of time, *per se*. The second is their own uncertainty with respect to their capacities and the possibility of their finishing. However, older persons are not unique in these respects. Every student faces these problems when choosing a program. The case histories and our interviews with university officials made strikingly clear the extent to which a bachelor's degree is seen as the "common school" for high study. Once one has the degree, everything else seems open. Deficiencies can be remedied by intermittent, part-time, or independent study.

On its face there is nothing particularly significant about four years of college, except that at that point one receives a recognized credential of accumulated education which becomes a kind of "open door" for many other fields. For many people, and this is particularly true for the potential older student, the indefinite status of one who has studied for some time without obtaining his credentials is particularly inhibiting. Movement upward by stages might be facilitated by providing some kind of a certificate at the end of each "feasible" unit of education, say, at the end of the first two years of college, at the bachelor's level, at the master's level, and probably at some level intermediate between the master's and the Ph.D. This would make it easier for those who reenter the education stream to start their trek to the next higher level.

Four-year colleges are already faced with the problem of the admissibility of graduates of junior or community colleges. It seems fairly clear that in the next decade or two senior colleges will be faced with the problem of the admissibility of middle-aged people who have a two-year degree and who want to obtain a full bachelor's degree. Two years to get a bachelor's degree is not too long for many middle-aged persons, and it will undoubtedly turn out that significant numbers of community college graduates will want to return to education in middle age.

It is clear that financial aid is crucial for potential middle-aged students whether they have high or low incomes. The expenditure-income balance seems to be precarious at all levels. As the case histories demonstrated, those with relatively little income often said that they had adequate financial resources to go to school, while many with relatively high incomes felt that they were inhibited in their educational choices because of other demands on them. People build standards of living into their lives according to their incomes, and it is difficult to reduce one's standard of living at any point in time.

It is also clear that the entire subject of the returns on educational investments to individuals and to society needs to be re-evaluated in relation to different groups of students and programs. Many admissions officers make the questionable assumption that young students will spend a longer time in their fields than older students. This study testifies to mid-career mobility, as does any study of the current employment of graduates of a particular program of, say, ten years ago. This is especially true with regard to women. The American population is so mobile with respect to occupation and irrespective of education that any calculation of the returns on education in particular fields needs to be carefully considered.

In particular, it is necessary to reappraise educational investments in women of different ages. Scarce educational resources may be invested in a young woman with relatively little return except of an indirect sort because of her imminent marriage and departure from the labor force. On the other hand, a relatively high proportion of middle-aged women students remain in their fields and give more years of service in return for the investment in their education.

Financial aid to mature students raises somewhat more fundamental questions, however. This study demonstrates that a great number of older students are in school for their own satisfaction. In other words, nonmonetary returns are often quite important in professional level employment. This does not mean that money is unimportant but that it is one among a great many influences and is by no means the most important. The question of how to measure these other returns and how to relate them to decisions about public investments in education is the point at issue here. In particular, there is a question of whether the public should be expected to provide a subsidy for graduate education which is primarily to satisfy personal or intrinsic needs of older individuals.

In this connection, however, nonmonetary returns are greatest for those who will be employed outside the private enterprise system. It is precisely in these areas that there are continued and expanding needs and shortages of personnel. Middle-aged students often seem to be responding to these needs, but their own needs are also important in their decisions to help perform a larger social service. It should also be noted that increased public demand for manpower in these fields is expressed not so much by expenditures for the services as by more funds for training to create a supply of trained manpower.

The problem of priorities among classes of students is likely to become more crucial in the future. The postwar baby boom which has been rolling through the educational system for nearly two decades hit the freshman year in college in about 1965 and the professional and graduate schools about four years later.

It is almost certain that in the early 1970s the number of potential applicants for graduate study will soar well above the number of places. In these circumstances, admissions officers can be expected to become more selective. They will tend to restrict their selections to the highly qualified, among whom, in their view, there are relatively few older applicants. Admissions officers can also be expected to raise more sharply the question of the advisability of admitting applicants whose expected work life or contribution to the profession may be marginal. This will work against not only older applicants but women as well and indeed anyone who shows evidence of uncertainty in his goals. Institutions with a surfeit of highly qualified applicants may take the easy way out and avoid the difficult problem of appraising older applicants by arbitrarily excluding them.

The fact that so many older students are in graduate and professional schools further confirms Louise Sharp's finding that there is no typical graduate student. Rather than a simple continuation of undergraduate education, she concluded, the pattern of graduate education is discontinuous, and extends over a long period of time. In fact, she concluded that the "deviant" student is the norm. She points out that many students are willing to pursue their studies "without concern for the traditionally appropriate age and family roles, [having] accepted the concept of a life-long interaction between work and study."[3]

Our study provided a number of clues that the role of the family in furthering higher education is changing. It is not uncommon for promising young women to abjure graduate school in favor of supporting their husbands while the latter are in school. Later, they may expect reciprocal support for their own study. This may be possible only after their children have reached a certain age. On the other hand, husbands and wives are under pressure to reenter and complete their studies before their

[3] Louise M. Sharp, "Graduate Study and Its Relation to Careers: The Experience of a Recent Cohort of College Graduates," *The Journal of Human Resources,* Vol. 1, No. 2 (Fall 1966), p. 58.

children start college or wait until their children's education is complete. Indeed, some wives return to school as a first step toward getting a good job so that they can contribute more to paying for their children's college study. Some wives return to work to support their husbands' return to graduate study in middle age. On the other hand, the return of some wives to school was eased by the affluence of their husbands. In a few cases, both husband and wife wanted to return to school, and decisions had to be made as to who would attend at what time. In some other cases, however, both husband and wife were able to get support and they attended school at the same time. Determining who in the family should go to school in successive years is an important question in a significant number of families.

In another context, Kenneth Keniston has argued that a great deal of the current student restlessness and questions of contemporary society "involve a continuing struggle against psychological or institutional closure or rigidity in any form, even the rigidity of a definite adult role. Positively [the new modes of thought] extol . . . the virtues of openness, motion and continuing human development. . . . There is emerging a concept of a lifetime of personal change, of an adulthood of continual self-transformation."[4]

This study provides evidence of the extent to which role definitions in middle age are less sharp. Middle-aged persons now have more freedom to define new goals. This seems to have been occurring for some time among women, although popular magazines portray the increased choices open to women in middle age as crises and dilemmas. The interesting note is that increased options at middle age also seem to be opening for men. Early marriage and small families mean a relief from some of the most pressing financial responsibilities of a home, educating one's

---

[4] Kenneth Keniston, "You Have to Grow Up in Scarsdale to Know How Bad Things Really Are," *New York Times Magazine* (April 27, 1969), pp. 128-129.

children, and the like, while one is still young. Significant numbers of men are able to satisfy their responsibilities and still set out to explore subjects of intrinsic interest to them or to escape from unsatisfying careers.

For these and many others, new choices or options are opening up. This fits in with the long-run trend to greater freedom of choice in American society in general. Of course people always have had choices, but there seems to be an expansion of the scope within which choices may be made. Choices are always difficult but they also represent an enlargement of freedom. In this sense, therefore, the return to full-time study for middle-aged men and women is simply more evidence of the long-run trend towards a better and a freer life for men and women in America.

Appendix Tables

TABLE A.1. Older Graduate Students, Respondents to 1963 National Survey

Field of Study	Students aged 35 or older as percent of all students, by sex			Females as percent of students aged 35 or older	Percentage distribution of students aged 35 or older, by sex		
	Total	Male	Female		Total	Male	Female
Physical sciences	*13*	*13*	*21*	*14*	*19.3*	*24.4*	*8.4*
Astronomy	11	11	8	8	1.0	1.3	0.2
Chemistry	9	8	17	23	1.9	2.2	1.4
Physics	8	8	6	3	1.4	2.0	0.1
Geography	22	20	32	21	4.3	5.0	2.9
Geology & geophysics	9	9	6	2	1.6	2.3	0.1
Oceanography	12	13	*	0	0.7	1.1	*
Metallurgy	13	12	*	4	0.9	1.3	*
Meteorology	22	22	*	2	2.0	2.9	*
Mathematics	13	11	23	32	2.5	2.5	2.6
General physical sciences	24	23	35	16	1.4	1.7	0.7
All other earth & physical sciences	16	16	8	2	1.6	2.3	0.1
Engineering	*12*	*12*	*21*	*1*	*16.3*	*23.6*	*0.5*
Civil engineering	13	13	*	0	3.2	4.6	*
Chemical engineering	6	6	*	2	1.6	2.3	*
Electrical engineering	14	14	*	0	4.3	6.3	*
Mechanical engineering	12	12	*	0	3.7	5.4	*
All other engineering	15	15	*	3	3.4	4.8	*
Life sciences	*13*	*11*	*22*	*36*	*30.0*	*28.2*	*33.9*
Anatomy	15	11	24	46	1.3	1.0	1.9
General biology	25	12	36	76	7.5	2.6	18.0

TABLE A.1. (*continued*)

Field of Study	Students aged 35 or older as percent of all students, by sex			Females as percent of students aged 35 or older	Percentage distribution of students aged 35 or older, by sex		
	Total	Male	Female		Total	Male	Female
Biochemistry	3	3	4	25	0.6	0.6	0.5
Botany	14	12	21	28	2.9	3.1	2.6
Biophysics	7	8	0	0	0.5	0.8	0.0
Genetics	11	13	5	9	1.2	1.6	0.3
Microbiology	13	12	16	43	3.3	2.7	4.4
Pathology	15	16	*	6	0.7	0.9	*
Pharmacology	12	10	27	26	1.0	1.1	0.8
Physiology	12	10	20	31	2.0	2.0	2.0
Zoology	10	10	10	24	2.3	2.5	1.7
Agriculture	12	12	*	0	2.0	3.0	*
Forestry	16	16	*	1	2.7	3.9	*
All other biology	13	12	22	23	2.1	2.4	1.5
Behavioral sciences	*18*	*14*	*31*	*43*	*17.2*	*14.3*	*23.6*
Psychology	14	8	28	59	3.5	2.1	6.6
Anthropology	20	15	28	52	4.4	3.1	7.2
Economics	20	19	29	13	4.9	6.2	2.0
Sociology	21	14	38	56	4.4	2.9	7.8
Humanities	*17*	*12*	*25*	*55*	*6.7*	*4.4*	*11.7*
English	19	10	28	75	3.6	1.3	8.7
History	14	13	20	31	3.1	3.1	3.0
Social work	*36*	*29*	*41*	*67*	*10.4*	*5.1*	*22.0*
Total	15	13	27	32	100.0	100.0	100.0

* Fewer than 10 female respondents of all ages.

Source: Seymour Warkov, Bruce Frisbie, and Alan S. Berger, *Graduate Student Finances, 1963*, NORC Report No. 103, (Chicago, 1965).

TABLE A.2. *Older Professional and Graduate Students, University of Chicago, Fall 1965*

School or Department	Students aged 35 or over as percent of all students	Females as percent of students aged 35 or older	Percentage distribution of students aged 35 or older, by sex		
			All[a]	Male[b]	Female[c]
Professional					
Divinity	12.1	12.8	8.6	13.3	2.6
Law	0.4	*	0.4	0.8	0.0
Medicine	0.4	*	0.2	0.4	0.0
Library service	26.6	52.0	5.5	4.7	6.7
Graduate					
Business	2.9	0.0	3.3	5.9	0.0
Education	5.4	80.0	2.2	0.8	4.1
Social service	11.0	67.6	7.5	4.3	11.9
Biological sciences	*5.8*	*27.8*	*4.0*	*5.1*	*2.6*
Anatomy	0.0	*	0.0	0.0	0.0
Biochemistry	0.8	*	0.2	0.4	0.0
Biology, general	0.0	*	0.0	0.0	0.0
Biophysics	0.0	*	0.0	0.0	0.0
Biopsychology	6.1	*	0.4	0.8	0.5
Botany	9.4	*	0.7	1.2	0.0
Mathematical biology	0.0	*	0.0	0.0	0.0
Microbiology	8.3	*	0.7	1.2	0.5
Paleozoology	20.0	*	0.4	0.8	0.0
Pathology	18.8	*	0.7	1.2	0.0
Pharmacology	4.3	*	0.2	0.4	0.0
Physiology	0.0	*	0.0	0.0	0.0
Zoology	5.5	*	0.7	0.0	1.5

School or Department	Students aged 35 or over as per-cent of all students	Females as per-cent of students aged 35 or older	Percentage distribution of students aged 35 or older, by sex		
			All	*Male*	*Female*
Humanities	*11.9*	*51.5*	*21.5*	*18.4*	*25.8*
Art	16.8	93.8	3.5	.4	7.7
Classical language & literature	5.1	*	0.4	.8	0.0
Comparative studies in literature	15.4	*	0.4	.4	0.5
English language & literature	6.6	68.0	5.5	3.1	8.8
General studies in humanities	1.3	*	0.2	0.0	0.5
Germanic language & literature	5.6	*	0.4	0.0	1.0
History	0.0	*	0.0	0.0	0.0
History of culture	15.4	*	0.4	0.0	1.0
Ideas & methods	10.7	*	0.7	1.2	0.0
Linguistics	12.1	*	1.6	1.6	1.5
Music	9.3	*	0.9	1.6	0.0
New Testament & early Christian literature	8.3	*	0.2	.4	0.0
Oriental languages & civilizations	14.0	16.7	2.7	6.4	1.0
Philosophy	3.8	*	1.3	2.3	0.0
Slavic languages & literatures	14.8	*	2.0	1.6	2.6
Romance languages & literatures	7.5	*	1.1	1.2	1.0
Field unchosen	0.0	—	0.0	0.0	0.0
Physical sciences	*1.6*		*1.8*	*2.7*	*0.5*
Astronomy & astrophysics	0.0	*	0.0	0.0	0.0
Chemistry	1.6	*	0.9	1.2	0.5
Geophysical sciences	1.6	*	0.2	0.4	0.0
Mathematics	0.4	*	0.2	0.4	0.0
Physics	0.3	*	0.2	0.4	0.0
Statistics	4.2	*	0.0	0.0	0.0
Field unchosen	0.0	*	0.0	0.0	0.0

TABLE A.2. (continued)

School or Department	Students aged 35 or over as per- cent of all students	Females as per- cent of students aged 35 or older	Percentage distribution of students aged 35 or older, by sex		
			All	Male	Female
Social sciences	*14.8*	*44.3*	*44.6*	*43.8*	*45.9*
Anthropology	4.7	*	1.6	1.6	1.5
Economics	2.6	*	1.3	1.9	0.5
Education (not graduate school)	37.9	46.7	26.8	25.4	29.4
Far Eastern civilizations	0.0	*	0.0	0.0	0.0
Geography	4.5	*	0.4	0.4	0.5
History	6.4	35.3	3.8	4.3	3.1
Human development	16.8	55.0	4.4	3.5	5.7
International relations	0.0	*	0.0	0.0	0.0
Political science	2.0	*	1.3	1.6	1.0
Psychology	3.7	*	1.6	1.9	1.0
Social thought	14.3	*	0.9	1.2	0.5
Sociology	5.7	50.0	2.2	1.9	2.6
Field unchosen	0.0	*	0.0	0.0	0.0
Total of above	8.7	43.1	100.0	100.0	100.0

* Less than 10 in total   [a]N = 450   [b]N = 256   [c]N = 194

TABLE A.3. *Older Professional and Graduate Students, New York University, Fall 1966*

School or Department	Students aged 35 or older as percent of all students, by sex			Females as percent of students aged 35 or older	Percentage distribution of students aged 35 or over, by sex		
	All	*Male*	*Female*		*All[a]*	*Male[b]*	*Female[c]*
Undergraduate professional schools	9.2	9.0	9.7	34	12.5	13.2	11.4
Engineering & science	5.2	5.5	*	1	1.8	2.8	*
Education	15.0	25.0	10.2	46	8.1	6.8	10.1
Commerce	5.9	5.5	9.8	18	2.6	3.4	1.2
Arts	1.2	1.9	*	*	*	*	*
Graduate schools and programs	22.8	19.6	30.1	39	83.1	80.8	86.9
Engineering & science	11.9	12.0	*	1	4.6	7.3	*
Arts & science	17.7	15.5	21.5	46	18.8	16.2	23.1
Education	36.7	30.9	36.9	52	38.7	29.7	53.7
Business	18.1	17.6	24.7	9	16.0	23.2	3.9
Public administration	27.9	26.5	37.3	18	2.4	3.2	1.2
Social work	34.4	31.4	35.8	70	2.5	1.2	4.7
Arts	5.0	0.0	*	*	*	*	*
Graduate professional schools	4.7	5.0	3.5	15	4.4	6.0	1.7
Law	8.5	8.1	14.8	13	4.2	5.8	1.5
Medicine	1.1	*	*	*	*	*	*
Nursing	0.0	*	*	*	0	0	0
Dentistry	0.5	*	*	*	*	*	*
Total of above	16.5	15.1	21.9	34	100.0	100.0	100.0

*Less than 10 in total   [a]N = 4,375   [b]N = 2,745   [c]N = 1.630

TABLE A.4. *Older Full-time Professional and Graduate Students, New York University, Fall 1966*

School or Department	Students aged 35 or older as percent of all students, by sex			Females as percent of students aged 35 or older	Percentage distribution of students aged 35 or older, by sex		
	All	*Male*	*Female*		*All[a]*	*Male[b]*	*Female[c]*
Undergraduate professional schools	*1.9*	*1.1*	*3.5*	*63.5*	*17.3*	*13.0*	*21.6*
Engineering & science	*	*	0.0	0.0	1.4	2.9	0.0
Education	4.1	4.2	4.1	73.3	14.1	7.7	20.2
Commerce	0.7	*	*	*	1.9	2.4	1.4
Arts	0.0	0.0	0.0	0.0	0.0	0.0	0.0
Graduate schools and programs	*7.2*	*5.2*	*12.0*	*49.7*	*77.5*	*79.8*	*75.2*
Engineering & science	2.1	2.1	0.0	0.0	2.3	4.8	0.0
Arts & sciences	3.9	3.5	5.1	35.4	18.5	24.5	12.8
Education	15.3	13.2	16.8	63.9	37.1	27.4	46.3
Business	2.4	2.1	*	*	3.5	6.3	0.9
Public administration	4.3	*	*	*	1.2	1.4	0.9
Social work	23.6	31.4	18.5	47.5	14.3	15.4	13.3
Arts	2.8	0.0	*	*	0.5	0.0	0.9
Graduate professional schools	*0.7*	*0.6*	*0.9*	*31.8*	*5.2*	*7.2*	*3.2*
Law	*	0.8	*	*	2.8	4.3	1.4
Medicine	*	*	*	*	1.4	1.4	1.4
Nursing	0.0	0.0	0.0	0.0	0.0	0.0	0.0
Dentistry	*	*	*	*	0.9	1.4	0.5
Total of above	3.7	2.5	6.4	51.1	100.0	100.0	100.0

* Less than 10 persons in total   [a]N = 426   [b]N = 208   [c]N = 218

TABLE A.5. *Older Professional and Graduate Students, Columbia University, Fall 1966*

School or Department	Students aged 35 or older as percent of all students, by sex			Females as percent of students aged 35 or older	Percentage distribution of students aged 35 or older, by sex		
	All	Male	Female		All[a]	Male[b]	Female
Health careers	*8.4*	*9.2*	*7.0*	*30.9*	*10.0*	*11.1*	*8.2*
Dentistry (incl. grad.)	9.3	9.6	*	0.0	1.7	2.8	0.0
Dental hygiene	23.3	24.1	18.2	9.5	1.9	2.8	0.5
Medicine	0.0	0.0	0.0	*	0.0	0.0	0.0
Occupational therapy	5.3	*	5.4	*	0.2	0.0	0.5
Physical therapy	7.1	*	5.9	*	0.3	0.2	0.5
Psychoanalytic clinic	25.0	22.5	*	10.0	0.9	1.5	0.2
Public health	36.0	32.5	42.0	42.9	4.4	4.1	5.0
Nursing	2.0	*	2.1	*	0.5	0.0	1.4
Other professional schools	*10.3*	*8.2*	*1.9*	*34.7*	*52.1*	*54.8*	*47.7*
Architecture	7.6	6.2	16.6	30.4	2.1	2.3	1.7
Business	4.1	3.8	17.4	9.1	4.0	5.8	1.0
Engineering	6.8	6.8	8.1	2.8	9.6	15.1	0.7
International affairs	4.9	4.4	6.1	*	0.7	0.7	0.7
Journalism	7.1	7.4	6.5	*	0.7	0.9	0.5
Social work	21.5	23.7	20.6	66.3	18.9	10.2	33.1
Law	1.0	0.7	5.6	*	0.8	0.9	0.7
Library service	39.2	41.0	33.3	19.4	14.1	18.3	7.2
School of the Arts	10.4	5.3	18.0	69.2	1.2	0.6	2.2
Graduate faculties	*11.0*	*9.3*	*14.3*	*44.1*	*37.9*	*34.1*	*44.1*
Humanities	*13.8*	*14.3*	*13.2*	*43.6*	*18.3*	*16.7*	*21.1*
East Asian language & culture	9.7	10.0	9.4	*	0.6	0.6	0.7

TABLE A.5. (*continued*)

School or Department	Students aged 35 or older as percent of all students, by sex			Females as percent of students aged 35 or older	Percentage distribution of students aged 35 or older, by sex		
	All	*Male*	*Female*		*All*	*Male*	*Female*
English & comparative literature	10.1	8.7	12.4	46.7	4.1	3.5	5.8
Art history & archeology	15.2	11.9	17.6	66.7	2.2	1.2	3.8
Germanic languages	26.2	25.0	27.3	54.5	1.0	0.7	1.4
Religion	18.8	15.9	25.0	41.7	1.1	1.0	1.2
Greek & Latin	11.3	10.3	12.1	*	0.6	0.4	1.0
Spanish & Portuguese	20.7	16.6	22.4	76.5	1.5	0.6	3.1
Italian	38.9	*	*	*	0.6	0.7	0.5
Linguistics	7.7	8.7	6.2	*	0.3	0.3	0.2
Music	13.0	10.8	15.6	*	0.8	0.6	1.2
Near & Middle East languages	13.6	7.7	22.2	*	0.5	0.3	1.0
Philosophy	11.3	8.5	20.0	42.9	1.3	1.2	1.4
French & Romance philology	16.2	11.1	19.2	74.1	2.5	1.0	4.8
Slavic languages	18.8	17.9	20.0	46.2	1.2	1.0	1.4
Political science	*11.3*	*10.9*	*12.4*	*33.1*	*15.1*	*16.2*	*13.2*
Anthropology	14.3	16.1	12.5	43.8	1.5	1.5	1.7
Economics	9.4	8.7	12.2	25.0	1.8	2.2	1.2
History	12.4	12.2	13.0	32.3	5.6	6.1	4.8
Mathematical statistics	4.7	5.5	*	*	0.2	0.3	0.0
Public law & govt.	11.0	11.0	11.0	26.1	4.2	5.0	2.9
Sociology	12.0	9.1	10.6	57.9	1.7	1.2	2.6
Social psychology	4.2	6.3	*	*	0.1	0.2	0.0

TABLE A.5. (*continued*)

School or Department	Students aged 35 or older as percent of all students, by sex			Females as percent of students aged 35 or older	Percentage distribution of students aged 35 or older, by sex		
	All	Male	Female		All	Male	Femal[c]
Pure science	*3.6*	*2.6*	*7.8*	*42.3*	*2.4*	*2.2*	*2.6*
Astronomy	0.0	0.0	*	*	0.0	0.0	0.0
Biochemistry	9.4	0.0	23.1	*	0.3	0.0	0.7
Botany	17.1	5.9	27.8	*	0.5	0.2	1.2
Chemistry	0.0	0.0	0.0	*	0.0	0.0	0.0
Geology	5.0	4.6	7.7	*	0.5	0.7	0.2
Mathematics	1.6	1.8	*	*	0.1	0.2	0.0
Pharmacology	18.2	*	*	*	0.2	0.2	0.2
Physics	0.6	0.6	*	*	0.1	0.2	0.0
Physiology	10.0	*	*	*	0.1	0.2	0.0
Psychology	4.6	5.0	4.0	*	0.3	0.3	0.2
Zoology	0.0	0.0	0.0	*	0.0	0.0	0.0
Electrical eng.	6.3	6.3	*	*	0.1	0.2	0.0
Other depts.	5.4	6.5	0.0	*	0.2	0.3	0.0
Joint committees	*8.9*	*17.3*	*16.2*	*26.1*	*2.1*	*2.5*	*14.4*
Chemical biology	0.0	*	*	*	0.0	0.0	0.0
Industrial & management eng.	20.0	20.0	*	*	0.2	0.3	0.0
Geography	23.7	24.1	*	*	0.8	1.0	0.5
Administrative medicine	27.3	*	*	*	0.3	0.2	0.5
Architecture, technology & planning	40.0	36.4	*	*	0.5	0.6	0.5
Other depts.	6.3	8.7	*	*	0.2	0.3	0.0
Total of above	10.3	8.7	14.8	37.9	100.0	100.0	100.0

* Less than 10 persons in total   [a]N = 1,101   [b]N = 684   [c]N = 417

TABLE A.6. *Older Professional and Graduate Students, Columbia University, including Teachers College, 1966*[a]

Students aged 35 or older as percent of all students

Columbia University proper	10.3
Teachers College	40.0
Columbia University, including Teachers College	20.4

Percentage distribution of all students aged 35 or older[b]

Total	*100.0*
Teachers College	66.3
Columbia University proper	
Health careers	*3.4*
Dentistry	0.6
Dental hygiene	0.6
Medicine	0.0
Occupational therapy	0.1
Physical therapy	0.1
Psychoanalytic clinic	0.3
Public health	1.5
Nursing	0.2
Other professional schools	*17.6*
Architecture	0.7
Business	1.3
Engineering	3.2
International affairs	0.2
Journalism	0.2
Social work	6.4
Law	0.3
Library service	4.8
School of the Arts	0.4
Graduate faculties, total	*12.8*
Humanities	*6.2*
East Asian languages & culture	0.2
English & comparative literature	1.4

TABLE A.6. (*continued*)

Art history & archeology	0.7
Germanic languages	0.3
Religion	0.4
Greek & Latin	0.2
Spanish & Portuguese	0.5
Italian	0.2
Linguistics	0.1
Music	0.3
Near & Middle East languages	0.2
Philosophy	0.4
French & Romance philology	0.8
Slavic languages	0.4
Political Science	*5.1*
Anthropology	0.5
Economics	0.6
History	1.9
Mathematical statistics	0.1
Public law & government	1.4
Sociology	0.6
Social psychology	0.0
Pure Science	*0.8*
Astronomy	0.0
Botany	0.2
Biochemistry	0.1
Chemistry	0.0
Geology	0.2
Mathematics	0.0
Pharmacology	0.1
Physics	0.0
Physiology	0.0
Psychology	0.1
Zoology	0.0
Electrical engineering	0.0
Other departments	0.1
Joint committees	0.7
Chemical biology	0.0

Industrial & management engineering	0.1
Geography	0.3
Administrative medicine	0.1
Architecture, technology, & planning	0.2
Other departments	0.0
Total	100.0

[a] Based on data for students attending Columbia proper in fall of 1966 who had been born in 1930 or earlier, plus Teachers College students attending in spring of 1966 and aged 35 or older.

[b] $N = 3,266$

TABLE A.7. *Older Full-time Professional and Graduate Students, Columbia University, Fall 1966*

School or Department	Students aged 35 or older as percent of all full-time students, by sex			Females as percent of students aged 35 or older	Percentage distribution of students aged 35 or older, by sex		
	All	Male	Female		All[a]	Male[b]	Female[c]
Health careers	*4.4*	*5.3*	*3.4*	*36.8*	*12.9*	*14.8*	*10.6*
Dentistry	4.8	4.9	*	*	1.8	3.3	0.0
Dental hygiene	0.5	*	0.5	*	0.2	0.0	0.5
Medicine	0.0	0.0	0.0	*	0.0	0.0	0.0
Occupational therapy	0.0	*	0.0	*	0.0	0.0	0.0
Physical therapy	7.1	*	9.1	*	0.5	0.0	1.0
Psychoanalytic clinic	27.0	29.0	*	10.0	2.3	3.7	0.5
Public health	34.3	31.1	39.5	44.1	7.7	7.8	7.5
Nursing	0.7	*	.7	*	0.5	0.0	1.0
Other professional schools	*4.4*	*2.6*	*13.5*	*50.9*	*39.1*	*34.8*	*44.2*
Architecture	2.1	1.7	4.8	*	0.9	1.2	0.5
Business	2.6	2.5	10.5	7.7	5.9	9.8	1.0
Engineering	0.7	0.8	0.0	*	1.6	2.9	0.0
International affairs	4.5	4.7	4.3	*	1.6	2.1	1.0
Journalism	7.1	7.4	6.4	*	1.8	2.5	1.0
Social work	15.1	21.1	13.1	65.1	14.9	9.4	21.6
Law	0.7	0.4	5.7	*	1.4	1.2	1.5
Library service	29.9	28.2	30.4	76.1	10.4	4.5	17.6
School of the Arts	4.9	6.4	0.0	*	0.7	1.2	0.0
Graduate faculties	*7.1*	*5.9*	*9.8*	*42.3*	*48.1*	*50.4*	*45.2*
Humanities	*9.8*	*7.5*	*11.6*	*52.0*	*22.1*	*19.3*	*25.6*
East Asian languages & cultures	10.2	9.7	10.7	*	1.4	1.2	1.5

TABLE A.7. (continued)

School or Department	Students aged 35 or older as percent of all full-time students, by sex			Females as per- cent of students aged 35 or older	Percentage distribution of students aged 35 or older, by sex		
	All	Male	Female		All	Male	Female
English & comparative literature	6.8	6.4	7.6	37.5	5.4	6.1	4.5
Art history & architecture	9.7	5.5	13.8	72.7	2.5	1.2	4.0
Germanic languages	25.0	28.6	20.0	*	1.4	1.6	1.0
Greek & Latin	2.4	0.0	4.8	*	0.2	0.0	0.5
Spanish & Portuguese	12.2	25.0	6.9	*	1.1	1.2	1.0
Italian	27.3	*	*	*	0.7	0.8	0.5
Linguistics	3.2	5.0	0.0	*	0.2	0.4	0.0
Music	11.3	6.3	19.0	*	1.4	0.8	2.0
Near & Middle East languages	13.8	5.9	25.0	*	0.9	0.4	1.5
Philosophy	5.8	4.9	9.5	*	1.4	1.6	1.0
French & Romance philology	12.8	7.9	15.5	78.6	3.2	1.2	5.5
Slavic languages	8.7	7.7	10.0	*	0.9	0.8	1.0
Religion	14.3	11.4	21.4	*	1.6	1.6	1.5
Other depts.	*	*	*	*	0.0	0.0	0.0
Political science	7.8	7.5	8.6	30.8	20.5	25.8	14.1
Anthropology	11.4	12.2	10.6	45.5	2.5	2.5	2.5
Economics	6.1	5.8	7.4	20.0	2.3	3.3	1.0
History	8.4	8.5	8.4	28.1	7.2	9.4	4.5
Mathematical statistics	3.2	3.6	*	*	0.2	0.4	0.0
Public law & government	8.2	8.2	8.0	24.1	6.5	9.0	3.5
Social psychology	0.0	0.0	*	*	0.0	0.0	0.0
Sociology	6.5	4.0	10.2	*	1.8	1.2	2.5

TABLE A.7. (*continued*)

School or Department	Students aged 35 or older as percent of all full-time students, by sex			Females as per- cent of students aged 35 or older	Percentage distribution of students aged 35 or older, by sex		
	All	Male	Female		All	Male	Femal
Pure sciences	2.1	1.3	5.6	50.0	3.2	2.9	3.5
Astronomy	0.0	*	*	*	0.0	0.0	0.0
Biochemistry	6.7	0.0	16.7	*	0.5	0.0	1.0
Botany	7.1	0.0	14.3	*	0.5	0.0	1.0
Chemistry	0.0	0.0	0.0	*	0.0	0.0	0.0
Geology	3.9	3.2	*	*	0.9	1.2	0.5
Mathematics	1.7	1.9	*	*	0.2	0.4	0.0
Pharmacology	10.0	*	*	*	0.2	0.0	0.5
Physics	0.0	0.0	*	*	0.0	0.0	0.0
Physiology	10.0	*	*	*	0.2	0.4	0.0
Psychology	1.8	2.7	0.0	*	0.2	0.4	0.0
Zoology	0.0	0.0	0.0	*	0.0	0.0	0.0
Other depts.	5.1	3.4	10.0	*	0.5	0.4	0.5
Joint committees	10.0	8.6	13.3	40.0	2.3	2.5	2.0
Chemical biology	0.0	*	*	*	0.0	0.0	0.0
Geography	10.7	13.6	*	*	0.7	1.2	0.0
Architecture, tech- nology & planning	40.0	*	*	*	0.9	0.8	1.0
Other depts.	9.7	4.5	*	*	0.7	0.4	1.0
Total of above	5.4	4.1	9.1	44.9	100.0	100.0	100.0

* Less than 10 persons in total   ᵃN = 443   ᵇN = 244   ᶜN = 199

Index

Admission policies, xi, 55-70; need for reappraisal of older applicants, xi, 140-41; age as factor, 58-70, 146; re-admission or credit for prior work, 59, 66; for faculty wives, 59-60; Ph.D. applicants, 60, 61-62; financial resources as factor, 60-61, 62; desire for life of scholarship as factor, 63-64; sincerity of interest questioned, 64; assessment of quality of applicant a problem, 64-65; qualifications generally higher for older applicants, 65-66; in religiously oriented schools, 68

American Association of University Women, 72

Anthropology, study of, 72, 152, 155, 159, 162, 165

Association of American Medical Colleges, 19, 77

Berger, Alan S., 16, 17

Biology, study of, 19, 151, 153, 160, 162, 166

Bloom, Benjamin S., 139

Business and management, study of, 3, 26, 69, 78, 153, 156, 157, 158, 161, 164

Career change: definition, viii; factors in and reasons for, ix, 5-9, 28-53, 100-01; more satisfying life, ix, xii, 6, 7, 8-9, 53, 98, 145, 147-48; rapid growth of professional people, ix, 4, 133; family life, ix, 5-6,

7, 29, 88, 93, 95-96, 146-47; early retirement, ix, 6-7, 136; manpower shortage, xi, 22, 67, 97, 138; need for long-range plan, xi, 75; specialization, 2, 8, 133; education for new profession, 2, 11-12, 44, 50, 98, 136; move upward in field, 2, 98; patterns of, 3-4; acquire new skills, 4, 5, 11, 12, 35, 37-38, 52, 53, 100, 134; change of attitude 9; occupational choice, 18-19, 101, 134-36; certain fields not feasible, 19; intrinsic interest, 28, 30, 53, 99, 100; development of ambitions, 28, 36, 100; life of scholarship, 33; job problems, 45, 136; motives generally positive, 52; problems on leaving school and adjusting to new situation, 83, 96-97; improve financial status, 100; *see also* Economic factors affecting career change; Education; Family life; Financial resources and funds; Institutions

Catholic institutions, 22, 68, 70, 80

Chemistry, study of, 18-19, 151, 154, 160, 162, 166

Columbia University, New Careers program, 69, 72

Danforth Foundation, 72

Davis, James, 16, 22

Dentistry, study of, 19, 156, 157, 158, 161, 164

Economic factors affecting career change: manpower shortage, xi,

167